A STORY OF MARRIAGE

W
H
E
N

*"Hope for moving
from brokenness
to breakthrough."*

MIKE AND WENDY PERRY

When A Story of Marriage is non-fiction.

Copyright © 2021 by Michael Edward Perry and Wendy Marie Perry

All rights reserved. No part of this publication may be reproduced, stored in a retrieval system, or transmitted in any form or by any means, electronic, mechanical, photocopying, recording, scanning, or otherwise, without the prior written permission of the authors.

When

A Story of Marriage

By: Mike and Wendy Perry

1. **Facebook:** @themarriageshop
2. **Instagram:** @the.marriageshop
3. **Business Page:** www.connectmovegrow.com

ISBN 9798665094304

Cover design by Wendy M. Perry

Printed in the United States of America

Independently published by: Mike and Wendy Perry

WHEN ~ A STORY OF MARRIAGE

CONNECT WITH *US!*

Mike and Wendy Perry

...giving thanks always and for everything to God the Father in the name of our Lord Jesus Christ, submitting to one another out of reverence for Christ.

A STORY OF MARRIAGE

WHEN

"Hope for moving from brokenness to breakthrough."

MIKE AND WENDY PERRY

Acknowledgement

To everyone who has loved us in our best and worst times. We are not possible without you.

And now these three remain: faith, hope and love. But the greatest of these is love.

1 CORINTHIANS 13:13

Introduction

Before you turn another page, we must warn you... This book will change you.

When was written for one purpose... Hope. In what? Hope in the power of prayer, love, and forgiveness to create, heal, save, and even transform a marriage–from both Mike's perspective and (on "the flip side") from Wendy's point-of-view. Choose either story as your start point. Either way, this book will take you on a remarkably revealing journey–actually...two journeys!

It's a peculiar idea that two people from different areas, different backgrounds, and different households could come together for a lifetime of marriage. Every couple that comes together adds two more ingredients to this complex recipe–flaws and brokenness. From the day two people meet, they show up with their own unique version of differences, flaws, and brokenness. The both of us certainly did. That is why we thought it was important for other married couples, or people considering marriage, to understand our *entire* journey, not only the polished version that depicts just what it looks like today.

To be honest, we would have preferred to write a different story. In many ways, our life stories are filled with memorable and inspiring moments. We have been blessed beyond anything imaginable. Then again, we have each disappointed others and ourselves more times than we would like to admit. It would be nice to create a catalog of tips, tricks, and steps that provide the "blueprint to the perfect marriage and a great life." People would certainly read it. Who doesn't enjoy a great story of love and success? The problem with that concept is the reality that the "perfect" love story would do little to provide hope to couples who really need it.

You see, no one escapes disappointment and failure—even in marriage.

Did we mention that this book will change you? The exact nature of change depends very much on where you find yourself today. Perhaps you've made assumptions about other people—or yourself—that you will now reconsider. On the other hand, you might have chosen to discard, ignore, or deny things that now demand your attention. You might even begin reading these pages and attempt to anticipate what comes next, only to have your assumptions completely dismantled. You will laugh, and you will cry. You will experience happiness and joy, and you will feel deep sorrow. It will be a bit of a roller coaster ride. Isn't that just like marriage?

After over two decades working in, through, and on marriage, we can say that we never could have anticipated the twists and turns this journey has taken. Better, worse, rich, poor—it's easy to take those vows in the beginning. "Better" and "rich"? Oh yes, we're all signing up for that! When things are going well, we tend to access our best selves more readily. We forgive more quickly. We love more generously.

Oh, but "worse" and "poor"? We are certain that those two are why vows are required in the first place! Vows are a verbal proclamation of commitment to another person, no matter what happens. There are situations that should wreck a relationship under normal circumstances, but marriage is not a "normal" circumstance. Marriage is a divinely ordained covenant—a mutual agreement to come together aligned with specific design that God has created for marriage—a special order that models a special relationship—that of God, Jesus Christ, and the church...the people of God. That type of marriage requires more giving than taking, more forgiveness than blame, and moving close when you want to run away. Marriage requires a decision to love, even when you cannot "feel" it in a moment. Hard work? Yes. But we love our job! We hope you do too. If you don't, our hope is that you will discover that you can find that place. Yes...even you.

As you finish reading this revealing story, it is likely that you will feel unsatisfied-maybe a little cheated. You will, no doubt, want the rest of the story. There is a possibility that you will want to re-write your own story, but feel that you need more tools and resources to do it. If so, then the next book in this series is for you, and it's coming soon!

This book is two stories in one! You can start with Mike's story by turning this page, or if you prefer to start with Wendy's story, turn to page 95. Whichever way you choose to start we invite you to read them both!

Let's start at the beginning...

When

His story.

Finding Myself.

When I was growing up, the idea of marriage seemed...complicated. Seemed like pretty-much everyone in the family did it when the time came. That time was usually around 20-something. Getting married was as much a part of adulthood as was getting a place to live, finding a full-time job, and purchasing a car to get you there. Getting married was just an expectation. But staying married was a little less than certain. At least, it seemed that way for staying *happily* married. In fact, I don't know if I had a concept of what a "happy" marriage was when I was growing up. My parents seemed happy much of the time. Would I say they had a *"happy"* marriage? There was a time when I thought my parents had the perfect marriage. They were young, good looking, and they seemed to be in love, despite those late-night arguments. I would eventually learn that being in love was not enough. And those late-night arguments...they signaled more trouble than I knew. The flaws would become apparent in time—not unlike so many other married couples we knew.

I have two sisters—one older and one younger. We would sometimes listen together when our parents argued. Those late-night arguments seemed normal to us. They were not pleasant to listen to. We cried sometimes, but outside of that, what could be wrong? After all, vacations remained intact, we went to church on Sunday mornings, we ate meals together, and the gifts flowed at Christmas. It was all good.

Through my childhood eyes, marriages just didn't seem to make it. Both sets of grandparents were separated permanently. I don't know if those were legal separations. I

Michael E. Perry

always assumed that the separations were informal—that each of them decided that they would be better off on their own and just made it happen. I would later discover more details of their stories and the circumstances leading to those separations. We were like most other families as it relates to marriage problems. That information is on a need-to-know basis, and children certainly do not need to know!

Across the rest of my limited world, marriage seemed to be a bit of a "mixed bag"—most seemed like they were going through the motions and just surviving the experience and each other. There were a few that seemed different—almost like they enjoyed each other and their marriages. In retrospect, the marriages that were in trouble appeared to be more often than not, and the few that seemed to thrive and survive also seemed to be that way more times than not. When separations and divorces came, there weren't many surprises, but there were a few. On occasion word would spread about that seemingly perfect couple who suddenly separated or divorced with no outward signs of trouble. If *they* didn't make it, did anyone else have a chance?

I found myself wondering how people remained in relationships that seemed to be so difficult to maintain. Why stay in a marriage, when there are constant questions about faithfulness, lack of trust, or doubts about the viability of the relationship? Why remain in a situation that seems to make the primary participants feel unhappy, bitter, stressed, and stuck? Those were the things that stood out to me. I have no idea why these things were any of my concern, even before my teens. Perhaps I was attempting to see my future life and was having difficulty painting myself into a picture painted on my imagination's torn canvas. I believe my canvas—the possibilities I saw for myself, based on what I had seen in others—was being created with everything I saw over the years. It was also being torn with every harsh exchange, family separation, and marital failure.

Like many married couples in crisis, my parents appeared whole, happy, and healthy on the outside, even when things were falling to pieces at home. What choice did they have? They were educated, young professionals with great careers and unlimited potential. A successful marriage was simply part of the package. By every measure, life should have been "perfect" for a child growing up in my situation. Middle class. Single family home. Big yard. Two cars. Dog. Dad even had a boat. A great lifestyle can certainly project the appearance of a healthy marriage, but it turns out that material things and outward appearance are poor predictors of marital health, success, or happiness.

Despite my parents' challenges, things seemed normal to me. My family considered me a peaceful child who enjoyed cartoons and football. I was nice, but I would crush you after the football was snapped! I didn't create much trouble at all. I spent much of my time with cousins because most of my extended family—grandparents, aunts, and uncles lived close by. Having family nearby was always a treat and became an important aspect of my childhood. On the other hand, there were elements of my childhood that I wouldn't consider a "treat" at all, but they would have profound impact on who I became.

Before I knew what self-image was, mine was being shaped by exposure to sexually explicit material and situations. Looking back, it is easy to see the sexually damaging nature of those moments. Exposure to a magazine with nude women. Just pictures. Perhaps a pornographic video or television channel. Just videos, not real people. A secret, stolen kiss by a young lady in the neighborhood who was many years my senior. Nothing more, though. Simulated sexual acts—mental and then physical.

Ultimately, I was exposed to things in childhood that altered the way I viewed the world, myself, and other people—especially girls. I never said anything to my parents. How could I? What would I say? I know that my behavior was inappropriate and wrong. My guilt and fear were strong. I couldn't see my behavior as anything but my fault. Like countless others, I was introduced to the world of sex by people who knew better—people who were supposed to protect me. I didn't see their failure. I only felt my guilt and shame. Speaking up and telling my parents, or anyone else who cared for me, was simply not an option. Besides that, the truth was that there was something about sexual attraction that I wanted to explore.

My internal war—mental and emotional—was underway before middle school. My "eyes were opened" and I was drawn to what I saw. I quickly noticed sexually-themed programming on television and books and wanted to see more. My attraction to girls grew (although still afraid to utter a word). In contrast, there were memories that I wanted to avoid, deny, and bury forever. I certainly planned to. I was embarrassed that I was coached to simulate sexual acts as a child. I was ashamed that I practiced that behavior more than once. I was confused about sexual attraction—who should I be attracted to? What did it mean when I felt attraction to the "wrong" person? Family member, neighbor, friend, etc.? Did that make me a bad person? Over the years, I would discover that there were more people than I could count who shared stories similar to my own. That was shocking to me. How could such a troubling history be so common?

Exposure to sexual ideas at an early age can be profoundly damaging and burdensome to a child. I wouldn't say that I experienced life as one who felt "damaged" or "burdened." But without question, there was impact on my life. My awareness of sexuality was acutely sharpened—especially my own. I noticed girls as objects of sexual attraction as a pre-teen. As I approached middle school, my attraction to girls was strong, but I remained profoundly uncertain of what to do with that attraction. I didn't know if the attraction I felt was normal or not. I didn't know what "normal" looked like. I didn't know what to think of myself. I saw my previous experiences as flawed and wrong—completely useless for figuring out how to carry myself in the presence of the opposite sex. As I reflect, it's difficult to believe that a child could or should know what "normal" looks like when learning to interact with the object of their attraction. In my case, that child had no idea that he could not or should not know. At that time, I had no experiences to compare my own to. My friends and family were not talking, and my parents were not even a consideration. Too risky. All I knew was that I was shy.

Among the personality traits I might have welcomed going into middle school, "shy" was not among them. It was the one characteristic that could end a relationship before it began. That's certainly how I saw it. By 7th and 8th grade, the contrast between my inner thoughts and outward reality could not be more distinct. I found myself attracted to the girls I thought were the prettiest and most popular in school. Most never knew it. I usually kept my distance and admired from afar, constantly grappling with what to say and what to do if I ever got up the courage. I walked into middle school with shame over past experiences and uncertainty of a new school environment and new people. A full complement of physical and emotional changes related to puberty topped off the recipe. To make matters worse, I had been fitted with braces for my teeth not long before beginning my first year in middle school.

When my two front teeth grew in during the early days of elementary school, it looked like I had extra-large adult teeth in a child-sized head! They extended outward and there was a gap between them. I was subjected to ridicule that was embarrassing and hurtful. More of my confidence disintegrated. My parents didn't see most of the ridicule, but they knew my teeth required treatment. By the time I began junior high school, I was in the first year of many in braces.

I was preoccupied with my clothing, because I had little of it, while other boys wore what seemed like new Adidas sneakers and fat shoestrings every day. "Fat" shoestrings were just that—extra-wide laces born of the hip hop culture and on the feet of every rap star in every rap music video in the early '80s. I thought that my classmates held an advantage over me because they had superior clothing. That seemed to add another layer to my problem with self-confidence and image.

Then one day, something strange happened. A young lady, who was a little older, began to walk home in the group I walked in. She would always ask me to be her boyfriend or come visit her. I was way too shy and embarrassed for all of that, but I remember one thing she said, even to this day...

"You are going to be so "fine" in high school."
My mind was racing.
Who...me?

I'm not exactly sure what that meant for that moment, but it gave me hope. It was a slight turning point. I began to see myself through different eyes. Shy still? Totally. But it's funny how a seemingly insignificant statement could have such profound impact. I wanted to believe what she said. It took a while, but eventually, I began to believe that someone could see me in that way.

During my high school years, my parents fluctuated back and forth between conflict and reconciliation. They separated for over one year at one point. My sisters and I had no idea what would happen with our parents, but like other children in our situation, we adjusted. Our parents tried certain things to help normalize life for us. Christmas is a great example. After the separation, the volume of gifts on Christmas day was astounding to us. The mountain of gift-wrapped boxes was thigh high and extended out across the entire room, spilling out of the doors on either side. We had to dig our way to the tree! My sisters and I always assumed that our parents felt guilty for separating and disrupting our lives. We made it work, though. We found our rhythm and adjusted to our new life until the next change. Even after my dad returned home, the Christmas gift haul remained ridiculous. We did not complain.

With dad back, life seemed better for a while. My parents appeared more connected—on the surface. What we could not see were the deep-rooted problems and unresolved pain that existed for both of my parents. Those issues would eventually re-emerge and destroy their marriage for good.

When I was in high school, my dad would sometimes drop me off at my summer job on the way to his office. One morning, not long after an epic argument he and my mother had, he offered me some marriage advice. His instructions were simple... "Pray and ask God to send you your wife. Do not try to do that yourself." My thought on that was immediate...

Nah...I got this one, Lord.

I believed in prayer, but I didn't know what I might get if I left it in God's hands. I knew what I wanted in a woman, and I knew what I did not want! She needed to have a certain look, a certain height, a certain weight, a certain attitude... I could not see how I could trust God with such a pivotal decision. What if He sent someone that

I had to adjust to? What if I had to accept some flaw? I decided that the discussion with God about my wife would have to wait, or perhaps never happen at all.

While in high school, I got a little taller, my teenage frame began to take shape, and my teeth got a little straighter. I joined the football team in my sophomore year. Before that, I had played "sand lot" football for years growing up and decided to try out for our neighborhood team—the Cowboys. After having one of my braces punch through my top lip during practice (I seemed to have forgotten my mouthpiece that day), I did not return to practice...ever. I quit. I quit because I was embarrassed and a little afraid. For several years, I was ashamed that I gave up without facing my fear and overcoming embarrassment. I remained ashamed until I returned to play on my junior varsity football team several years later in high school. I didn't want to get comfortable with the idea of quitting. I resolved to never quit at anything again.

As I grew physically taller and stronger, my confidence grew as well. I was a starter on the football team, I had a few people I considered good friends, and I started dating a girl on the cheering squad. My braces came off, and my body was developing around my 6-foot frame. I was finding my stride. My shy personality was giving way to a growing belief that I might be able to build normal relationships and a normal life. I considered the possibility that I might be no more flawed than anyone else. My clothing mattered less. My attraction to women was more aligned with my stage of development. It didn't seem as disorienting. Still, hints of insecurity and uncertainty lingered. Having a girlfriend for several years quieted the doubt I carried about how desirable or valuable I might be. For the moment, I had enough, and life was good.

I thought I might marry my high school girlfriend at some point. We certainly talked about it. I figured I would get a football scholarship to somewhere, get a college degree, find a good job, and wait for my girlfriend, who was one year behind, to graduate college the following year to join me so that we could get married and start a family. Easy.

The scholarship plan I envisioned collapsed before it fully took shape. I was a solid football player with respectable grades and a strong SAT score. Despite participating in the "gifted" program in elementary school, I did not achieve my academic potential in high school. I could do most of my work and pass most tests with minimal preparation—usually a quick read or scan was all it took. I was satisfied to straddle the line between honors and mediocrity, pulling off a passing performance when the moment required me to step up. In contrast, my older sister who was a couple of years ahead of me and was near the top of her class. She graduated with honors and a prestigious full scholarship. Her footsteps were difficult to follow, so I just reasoned that I would create my own path. I knew that football would help me pave the way, but had no idea how.

Going into senior year, we had a new coach. I was working harder than ever and learning new skills to improve my game. I was even learning a new position—outside linebacker—and having amazing practice sessions going into the summer before the season began. I couldn't wait to get on the field and start the season. In one afternoon, everything changed forever.

Summertime meant two-a-day practice sessions—an early morning practice and an evening practice during the most brutally hot part of the summer. By late August, we were in the last days of summer practice sessions. I felt like I had earned a break. I picked a day when I would skip the afternoon practice, hang out with my girlfriend, and maybe grab something to eat. When I told my fellow seniors my plan, I got the immediate guilt-trip about our responsibility as team captains, "leading by example," and everything else

Michael E. Perry

I was reluctant to hear on that day. I knew how to lead by example, but I still wanted what I wanted. As the practice time got closer, my thoughts grew louder...

Do the right thing, Mike.

I decided to attend practice. I was having one of those days when it all comes together. I was in "the zone." I was a step ahead on defense, making my opponent look bad time after time. My primary opposition that day, was an underclassman tipping the scales at nearly 300 pounds. He was big, strong, and quick. He was a "man-child." On this day, I was quicker. I got the upper hand on yet another play, and coach had seen enough.

He...was...HOT. He screamed at man-child for getting out-played and staged the football equivalent of a duel. Just me, man-child, and a whistle as the team looked on. No one had to ask what this was. It was an attempt to shame my teammate into better performance. Shame is a poor performance enhancer—feedback and preparation are better. Nevertheless, there we were. Squared off, in our stances and waiting for the whistle. Our instructions?

"You against him. On the whistle." We instinctively knew what to do.

Our job was to clash and tussle until the sound of the next whistle. My best techniques were lightning quick and violent—essential for a 180-pounder whose job is to clash with linemen 100 pounds heavier. Hit fast and be gone. That had a way of pissing people off. So, there I was...my technique achieved the desired impact, but now I had two hands clamped under man-child's shoulder pads with no place to go. I would normally have been gone in seconds, but the job was to tussle. He recovered. With a grunt and the power of 300 pounds of dense, pissed-off football player, he got me on my heels, and I began to fall backward...never releasing my grip on those shoulder pads.

There was a snap. When he got up, I lifted and looked over at my left arm, twisted and broken. I watched it dangle for a second and had to lay down and look away. The pain was unlike anything I had experienced. A few hours later I was in surgery. What I thought would be my best season...the season that would lock in my scholarship opportunities...was over before it started.

After my injury, my college prospects quickly melted away. About 8 strong prospects dwindled to 2— Randolph Macon—a small school north of Richmond, Virginia, and The U.S. Naval Academy. I chose Navy. Because of my hunger to play football again, my decision-making process was simple.

They want me to play football? Check.
Full ride? Check.
Cool looking Naval Academy uniforms? Bonus.

I was in. I went through the process of applying and interviewing. I was accepted into the Naval Academy system and assigned to the Naval Academy Preparatory School (NAPS), in Newport, Rhode Island. The prep school was generally for students who needed to strengthen some area of performance—usually academic or athletic—before attending the Naval Academy in Annapolis, Maryland. I needed both. One fateful day at football practice had completely changed the trajectory of my college plans. Little did I know that moment would shift the trajectory of my entire life.

The Naval Academy Prep School (NAPS) was in Newport, Rhode Island, almost 600 miles from my childhood home. There were only a few high school graduates in my area who attended college out of state. Fewer, still, traveled as far as I had. My parents created an entire experience around my drop-off day in Rhode Island.

Michael E. Perry

They planned a family vacation to New York City and Niagara Falls, placing us within easy driving distance of Newport. My mother, father, two sisters, niece, and I packed into my father's van and off we went. We visited some iconic landmarks and took epic pictures, including the Statue of Liberty and the New York side of Niagara Falls. It was a great trip, but as we drew closer to my first day at NAPS, I felt a growing sense of dread. I had never been so far away from home for as long as I soon would be. And although my family shared the journey as we approached that day, I would have to complete the rest of the journey on my own.

On the morning I was scheduled to report to school, I was having second thoughts. I knew there was no turning back, but I did have a fleeting thought or two...

Maybe there will be a mix-up and my name won't be on the list...

We arrived in the school parking lot and found a row of long tables, each with several stacks of documents, organized in alphabetical order by last name. My name was on the list.

I knew my experience in the Naval Academy system would be much different than my friends in traditional college institutions. "Different" was an understatement. I hugged and kissed my family and lined up with several of my future classmates. We were led into the building where the "move in" process was already underway for those who reported earlier. It was chaos. If I had any doubts that NAPS is a school within a MILITARY academy system, this was my wakeup call.

The people in charge—"cadre"—were barking orders. The new students were doing push-ups, shouting incomprehensively, shuffling through the corridors, carrying bags from room to room, and other seemingly

When: His Story.

random and frantic activities. I was completely disoriented. This was my introduction to the indoctrination phase of the program. I thought of my family, only minutes down the road, and my friends who were still at home on summer break. I began to wonder if I'd made the right decision. Some students quit on the spot. In the first hours, they were on their way back home. For me, that wasn't an option. The only way out was through. No plan B.

Navy Prep delivered pressure far beyond what I had experienced in my life. I was forced to endure discomfort, pain, push-ups, early days, late nights, non-sensical rituals, crammed showers, and mealtimes with little time given to actually chew and swallow. We were constantly being hurried to whatever was next. For the first several weeks, I wanted to quit every day—every hour. I kept forcing myself to take another step and get through another day. I was learning resilience and discovering what I was capable of. Indoctrination ended, and the academic school year began. Monday through Friday, a full college class load, football practice, and weight training consumed my life. We were not allowed to leave the school grounds during the week. On the weekends, we were given "liberty." That's Navy-speak for freedom!

Within a few months, weight training and tough conditioning had added over 30 pounds of muscle to my frame. I successfully played football again, although I never fully regained the competitive edge and effortless instinct I enjoyed prior to my injury. Playing competitive football requires complete focus on the game you are playing, not on potential injury. I was having difficulty getting my mind off of avoiding injury and on to playing with reckless abandon as I once did. My football days were over, and I was at peace with that. Because my primary motivation for attending Navy was the opportunity to play football, I decided my Naval Academy journey would end as well. I applied for an Army Reserved Officer's Training Course

Michael E. Perry

(ROTC) scholarship, which would finance the remainder of my college education in exchange for 4 years of service as an Army officer. NAPS did not support my decision, but there was little they could do to stop it. If all went according to my new plan, the end of the school year would be the end of my Navy career. At the same time, my relationship with my girlfriend back home faded, and I began focusing on my next relationship. Dating between fellow "Napsters" was generally frowned upon by our leaders, but that didn't stop anyone. It certainly didn't stop me.

The winter in Newport was brutal for me—distinctly harsher than the southeastern Virginia winters I had grown accustomed to. As the cold winter season released its grip, only a few more months remained before the end of the school year and my return to normal life. Things were going as well as I could have hoped, but the weekday restrictions had become tiring. A few friends and I decided we would visit a local club on a Thursday night—a serious violation of school policy. Three of us crafted a plan, quietly slipped out and had a pretty good time on the town. We returned to our building and back to our rooms, undetected. We pulled it off! But there was one problem. A good friend of ours knew that we violated the rules, and he was feeling the weight of the code we all took—The Honor Code.

The Honor Code is a set of values that every service academy student is required to live by. The basic premise of the honor code is that "a midshipman candidate" (that's what we were) "does not lie, cheat, steal, *nor tolerate those who do.*" That "tolerate those who do" part had our good friend in a bit of a bind. He decided to do the right thing...and it was indeed the right thing. He reported our violation. For two of us, the end of our year came very quickly. I had two choices: go through "Captain's Mast"—a trial system for regulation violations—or turn in my request for disenrollment and discharge from the Navy. My football coach knew I had a scholarship in my pocket, the harsh plans for my punishment, and that I had no intent of continuing to Annapolis. "I recommend you get out and move on with your life...now," he said. He recommended I quit. That was a devastating moment. I had put so many years into persevering and overcoming insecurity and doubt. How could I now quit to avoid the consequences of my actions? The possibility of extended punishment through the summer sealed it. I knew I had to report to enroll at my next school, Norfolk State University, during the summer. I could not chance disrupting my new start. I submitted my withdrawal request from NAPS with about 6 weeks to go until the end. I was ordered to pack my bags and leave my room immediately. Next was "the walk of shame," as I carried my belongings past people I had grown to love in many ways. There were many tears and lots of hugs. The last person I reached was my good friend who reported our violation of the rules. He felt guilty...crushed. As he sobbed, I reassured him that he did the right thing. "It's okay."

    As I walked out, I felt profound sadness. For him. For me. For my girlfriend who had to witness this embarrassing turn of events. Less than 24 hours removed from my night out, my bags were packed, and I was being transported to the "holdover" barracks, where disenrolled students were housed. The room was a long open bay with a few dozen bunk beds on either side—probably about 100 beds total. Besides me, there was one other person in the entire room. I felt more alone than at any point in my life that I could remember. It was a hard day, but the most difficult moment was still to come. I had to call my parents.

    I grabbed the payphone handset at the end of the hallway to call home. My mother picked up. I could barely speak..."I have to come home. I got kicked out."

Michael E. Perry

Nine months earlier, I left home on a wave of fanfare and celebration. Everyone was so proud. Even after I'd won the ROTC scholarship, we were all silently holding out to see what might happen at year's end. No one expected the year to end like this. My mother gave my father the phone. "I have to come home."

I expected a speech. I received comfort and acceptance. My dad seemed to know that I had suffered enough for that day. My parents stepped up and provided me with the love, grace, and hope I needed in that moment. A few weeks later, my father was in Rhode Island to pick me up. We got on the road and didn't stop until we were arrived back in Portsmouth. The Norfolk State chapter was about to begin.

After a year in a military environment, I welcomed life on a normal college campus. I lived in a dormitory room with two roommates, that seemed a bit crammed to me, but I had few complaints. Army ROTC training was one day each week. Besides that, there were no marching formations. No uniforms. No restrictions. And there were lots of girls. I planned to remain faithful to my girlfriend from NAPS, but that would prove very difficult over time. Despite my failure back in Rhode Island, I was feeling confident about my future at NSU. After surviving the previous year's adversity, I believed that I could do anything, and I was determined to prove it. There could be no room for hesitation or insecurity, even if I felt it. If I wanted to do something new, I was going to try it, and if I wanted to meet to a young lady, I was going to speak to her.

I had no idea how women would respond to me at this point, but I learned that confidence is appealing—maybe even more so than looks! Whenever someone responded positively to me—my jokes, my smile, my conversation—I felt a little boost. When I discovered that, I poured it on, even when I felt uncertain. My list of telephone numbers grew rapidly. I started with a small black book and then random pieces of paper stuffed into an old peanut can. That container overflowed. I lived like I had something to prove—like I was still looking for someone or something that would finally help me feel like I had overcome that hint of insecurity that seemed to linger, no matter what I did. I wanted that boost, and I chased it, repeatedly. As months passed, I struggled to maintain my long-distance relationship. I just fell away. I felt guilty, but my guilt did not stop the momentum that was building. I had cracked the code. Women "saw" me and responded to me. I liked it. I thought I was under control. I was not.

My mother hardly ever meddled in my love life, but she made it clear that she disapproved of my dating activity. She thought there were too many girls. She always thought that I "enjoyed the chase." I was defensive and rejected her assessment of my motivation, but she wasn't completely wrong. I enjoyed the chase and the connection. I was uncertain of what I was really chasing. I was not always after sexual relationships, but I was not always opposed. One boundary was easy to create. If I thought someone seemed too emotionally close or exceedingly motivated to create a long-term exclusive relationship, I tried to pull back. It was my feeble attempt to protect unwitting women from falling in love and getting their feelings hurt by me.

Keeping my dating activity private and maintaining my schedule became a challenge—almost a full-time job. I didn't necessarily want these ladies to think they were merely one of many, but I was usually careful not to give false hope about long-term relationships. No need to get too close. I thought that would weaken my appeal, but it did not seem to. In fact, honesty was apparently as valuable and attractive as confidence was. The flood gates were open, but it still wasn't enough for me. Evidently, my need for connection and validation continued to run deep. It was a need that no single woman could fill. In fact, no person or

Michael E. Perry

number of people could solve my problem. Yes...it was a problem, but I didn't realize it then.

It took over a year in college for me to settle on a major course of study. I registered for an Introduction to Psychology class, as an experiment, to see if it would be a good fit for me. The content resonated and the professor made it interesting. I declared psychology as my major. I was going to become an Army Psychologist, and that path meant that a doctoral degree was my only option. Anything short of a Ph.D. would disqualify me from serving as a psychologist. I was researching my graduate school options when I discovered that the Department of Defense had a clinical psychology training program at the Uniformed Services University of the Health Sciences (USUHS), in Bethesda, Maryland. There was one notable catch—only one student each from the Army, Navy, and Air Force was granted admission for each class year. All I had to do was serve for five years, do great work, and apply for the single Army slot. What could go wrong? The odds seemed slim, and I had little information on how I would make it happen. One thought pressed me forward.

Why not me?

Time would tell. After my third year at NSU, I requested placement in the Army Medical Service Corps (MSC)—the first step in beginning my Army career and positioning myself for that single, graduate school seat when the time came. Several months before graduation, I got the news. I was going to be an Army MSC officer.

After graduation, I was off to Fort Sam Houston in San Antonio, Texas, for the Army Medical Department Officer Basic Course (OBC). The basic course was more military "class" than military "training"—about 3 months long. NAPS and ROTC prepared me well, and my time in San Antonio felt like a vacation. I spent my free time visiting new places, like the San Antonio Riverwalk. Soon after arrival at OBC, each of us was required to submit our top five preferences for first duty assignments. I requested places like Germany, Korea, and other locations considered good developmental assignments for young officers. After about 2 months, I received a letter—known as "orders"—notifying me of my first duty assignment—the first base and first job I would have as an Army officer. I was assigned to Walter Reed Army Medical Center (WRAMC) in Washington, DC...the world's largest military medical facility. My mind raced...

What?! Is somebody playing games with me?

I did a "double take" and read the memo twice. An assignment to Walter Reed made no sense. I didn't know that a Second Lieutenant (the rank at which most officers enter the military) could get Walter Reed as a first assignment. Otherwise, I might have actually asked for it! I imagined myself in the "Chocolate City" (a nickname made popular by DC-area radio disc jockeys and musicians in the 1970s, for its high population of African Americans...and for me, high population of successful black women). I gladly accepted my assignment. A good friend recommended that I reject the assignment and ask for Korea. I ignored his email.

I arrived at Walter Reed to discover I would be the administrator for the department of psychiatry.

How lucky could I get?!

At least, that was my first thought. My goal was to become a psychologist, so this could only be a good thing, right? My office was modern, well equipped, and located in the newest building at Walter Reed. My window was

Michael E. Perry

massive, providing a full view of lush campus grounds, immaculate landscaping, and an ornate fountain situated in the middle the grounds.

Not bad for your first real job, Mike. Pretty fancy!

After only a few days, I was transferred to a different job and a different office. My department chief suddenly had a vision for the future of the department, and I was not in it. Instead, I was placed in the oldest building at Walter Reed—"Building 1," a re-purposed early 20th century structure that opened its doors as Walter Reed General Hospital in 1909. My new office? I'm certain it was designed for utility or storage and converted later for administrative use. My view? An interior courtyard area paved for parking and flanked on four sides by the building's brick walls. There was a single tunnel for entry and exit. This was not new, nor was it fancy. For a moment, I prepared myself for the possibility that my military career was over before it began. This felt like moving backward. I didn't know it, but that move didn't destroy my career. My life and career were about to race forward in ways I could not imagine.

My new role was Deputy Director for Performance Improvement and Risk Management. I had no idea what I was doing, but I was willing to learn...and I did. The best thing about the role was exposure. My office was effectively a renovated closet, but outside of that closet, my position required that I maintain a high profile. I facilitated mandatory training every month in the hospital theater. That opened the door for me to be noticed and recommended for a new position that would be opening soon. I landed an interview with the Hospital Commander. He was looking for an assistant, known in the military as an Aide-de-Camp—a personal executive aide for general officers. I won the job. My responsibility was to ensure that everything related to the general's business was handled smoothly and professionally. Having this assignment in the nation's capital was a unique experience, particularly at such an early point in my career—less than two years from my first day at Walter Reed.

Military aide-de-camp is considered a prestigious position—an early indicator of potential for promotion to the highest levels of military leadership. I met politicians, entertainers, top level pentagon leaders, diplomats, and other VIPs from around the world. I also received information about opportunities I hadn't previously considered. I even entertained the possibility of attending pilot school to fly Army medical evacuation helicopters. Not my original plan, but I thought it might be fun to fly. I began the application process and got close, but flight school was not to be in my future.

After over a year in D.C., my experience had exceeded my expectations going in. Life was about as good as I dared to hope for at that point. Career options I once thought unreachable were emerging. I had a prestigious job, an amazing commander, a nice car, nice apartment (complete with a wood-burning fireplace!), lots of friends, and lots of love prospects. I was busy, but I found time to work on my social life. I would even cook dinner for my neighbors— the young ladies that lived a few doors down. I wasn't actively in pursuit of them, I just wanted to set the stage... "open the door," just in case someone wanted to walk through it. That was my way...

No pressure, but if you're down for whatever, I'm down for whatever.

At one point, I thought I might be ready to settle in with a long-term girlfriend. Everything seemed just right. She was attractive, successful, and really into me. She even laughed at my corny jokes. I thought maybe she was the one.

Why not?

I envisioned myself in *that* place. Settled, faithful, happy, and content with one woman. I could not remember the last time I allowed my imagination to go there, but there it was. I reflected on who I was...who I had been for so many years. Would I have anything new to offer this woman after giving so much of my time and myself to others? My plan was to get answers to that question by allowing myself to cultivate the relationship. And I did. There's one detail I neglected to account for: her previous boyfriend. I thought this guy was old news. Apparently, he was simply on pause...living in another city and strategizing a triumphant return. He had a few things I didn't have—money being tops on the list. And he had history with her. Until the moment he pulled a surprise visit, I had convinced myself I was impervious to heart break. I had no idea what it felt like...until I did. He showed up, she saw him, and I faded from her sight in seconds. At least, that's what it felt like.

For the first time, I felt deep emotional pain related to a relationship. I could not change anything about the situation, and I couldn't escape the reality. My feelings were hurt, and my ego was damaged. I felt embarrassed. I had allowed myself to peek forward into a future that was obviously not mine. My thoughts went into overdrive...

You look like a fool, dude.
How could I just disappear like that?
How could I have thought this was more than it was?

I reflected on how I managed to fall into this situation. Their relationship was clearly alive, even if damaged. I had to accept that quickly. Given the number of women I had disappointed at this point in my life, I reasoned that I probably deserved some pain of my own. I tried to turn the page and recover—get back to my old routine. This chapter was over. Or so I thought.

It took several months for me to feel like myself again, but in time, I was back to living my single life. Work, go out with friends, go on dates, meet new girls...repeat. This was the life I envisioned when I received those orders in San Antonio. I was now living it, but the thrill was waning. I was spending more time at home and less time out on the town. More time reflecting and less time chasing. I could not shake the idea that I might have given too much...and taken too much in my dating life. Why did I need these women in my life? What did I have remaining to offer my future wife that she could call her own? If the women I was dating were not going to my wife, why continue to experience moments that were not mine to have? I wasn't accustomed to asking myself deep questions like this. It was mentally exhausting.

My dating life began to stall, but I found myself going through the motions because the motions were familiar and within my comfort zone. The motions also left me feeling increasingly empty. Suddenly, I was emotionally tired. I wanted something different. There was companionship available to me if I wanted it, but my previous standard of companionship was no longer acceptable. I was suddenly overwhelmed with the sense that I was completely out of place.

I arrived home after work on a spring day to find an answering machine full of messages, mostly from young ladies asking me to call back. I listened to the first message. I had no interest...delete. Next message, and then another. Delete. Another. Delete. After several more messages, I was at my limit. I deleted every message. That very moment, I decided I would no longer spend a minute of my time talking to or spending time with anyone who was not "her"—the woman meant for me. I could not give another piece of myself away. I wanted something of value—something exclusive—available to offer my future wife, and I wanted her to believe that she was receiving something...someone who was valuable. It became painfully clear to me: I was designed to be with one woman. After everything I had been through and all I had done, I was a one-woman-man! I had idea where she was, who she was, or how to find her. As if the Holy Spirit was waiting for me to reach that moment, my father's words returned to me...

> *1 Corinthians 13:11*
> *When I was a child, I spoke like a child, I thought like a child, I reasoned like a child. When I became a man, I gave up childish ways.*

"Pray and ask God to send your wife."

I had intentionally ignored that advice since my early teens. On this day, I decided to take my dad's advice. I stopped in place, and prayed, right there on the floor in my apartment. Although I had lived my entire life with a detailed list of "must-haves" for my ideal woman, I didn't give God much of a description that day...

I will trust you to send the woman that you have chosen for me. I will recognize her, and I will say 'yes.'

That was it. I got up, ate dinner, and went to bed. The next day, it was back to work, just like always. Considering my lifestyle and decisions until that day, I had no reason to believe that my prayer was heard. I knew I didn't deserve an answer, but my mind was made up.

I was ready to show God that I could be trusted with something precious, and I was willing to wait to receive it.

Did you see anything you recognize?

In this chapter, you were invited to witness the complicated making of a young man—one perspective on how early experiences play out in life over time. The parts of ourselves that we expose to other people are usually polished parts we allow the world to see. The interior can be much messier. Know that none of us escapes brokenness. For so long, I didn't even know I was broken and lost. When I met Wendy, I was on a path toward healing. I was finding myself, but the process was only beginning. As you reflect on the beginning of my story, I encourage you to stop here and take some time to reflect on your own.

Michael E. Perry

When I Met her.

Focusing exclusively on work and myself outside of a relationship was an odd place for me. For years, it was about being on the hunt or in a relationship. At this point, I was simply on pause. I can't say, with honesty, that I was waiting for my prayer to be answered. I figured I might have to wait another year...5 years...10 years. Who really knew? I was just going through the motions, but in a different way this time. Career focus. Get to work on the next thing.

My office was in the hospital command suite, which was sectioned into 3 areas. The main area was a large administrative space with several sectioned-off work-spaces—one for each of the hospital's deputy commanders and Sergeant Major and a sitting area for guests. Within that main area was the entrance to the commander's support team office. I shared that space with the Commander's executive assistant. The third space was the Commander's office—a massive area almost as spacious as the first two combined. My desk was just inside the glass double doors of the support team office. I had clear view of everyone entering and leaving the command suite.

About two weeks after the evening I prayed for God to send me the woman who would be my wife, I was sitting at my desk typing an email...a fairly routine day. That's when it happened...

I caught a glimpse of two people entering the command suite main entrance. No big deal. That door probably opened 100 times a day. In an instant, the pair was entering my door. The first, I recognized as Leeah, a nurse working on our executive ward—the mysterious "Ward 71." That wing of the hospital was designed for senior

When: His Story.

government officials. It is without question, the most unique (and secure) space I have ever seen in a hospital—truly another world.

Leeah was accompanied by a young lady I had never seen. I figured she must be new. My old, well-rehearsed mindset kicked in...

Obviously, she is new. No way I missed this one.

She was...disarmingly beautiful. She was petite. I mean really petite. I figured she had to be under 5 feet tall. Quite tiny for a "Soldier." This was no ordinary Soldier though. Her presence was enormous—pure energy, to me at least. But not in a loud and boisterous way. She just filled the room by standing there. That's it. Her skin was a smooth cocoa brown, and she had a short, perfectly styled haircut. When we were introduced, I played it cool. I definitely felt *something*. I could not fully place it, but it was there. And then there was her smile. It just lit up the room. It was captivating. This girl had it all together. As it turns out, she had been working on the pediatric ward the entire time I had been at Walter Reed.

How had I missed this one?

Her name—1LT Wendy Underwood. She was as put-together as she was beautiful. I considered myself a squared away soldier—more so than most. She impressed *me*. That was not an easy feat. I'm just sayin'.

Leeah made introductions. "1LT Underwood, this is 2LT Perry, the General's aide." She went on, "1LT Underwood is just starting on Ward 71 and I'm introducing her to all of the important people."

Important people, I thought. *Well, you have come to the right place.*

"Hello," I said. "Nice to meet you. Please let me know if there is ever anything, I can do for you."

The intros were quick—maybe 5 minutes. It seemed like an hour. As they departed and she walked out of the door, I caught a glimpse of her profile. She was smiling HARD as she rounded the corner. Joyce was the Commander's executive assistant and my guide through the finer points of working for a commander. I adopted her as my godmother. Joyce probably went with it because she knew that I was a young man in need of some real, spiritually grounded support and a LOT of prayer. She was genuine, kind, and really funny.

As Wendy Underwood exited and walked down the hallway, I looked over at Joyce and said, "She wants me. Look at her smiling. I think she's digging me."

I was struck by the interaction with 1LT Underwood that day. So much so, that I talked to my dad later that evening. As I stood in my living room, staring blankly at the Buffalo Soldier painting on my wall, I shared with him that I had met a young lady who I thought was interesting. There *was something* about her. Suddenly, my career wasn't the only thing on my mind.

I was intrigued by 1LT Underwood, but I did not pursue her. I was still in a bit of life clean-up mode and I wanted to make sure I didn't get caught up in any of my old habits. I was willing to take a wait-and-see approach.

The work continued and I had career goals, so I was off to Airborne School to jump out of airplanes. Although Airborne school was only a few weeks long, it took only that long for me to somewhat re-complicate what I had managed to make a relatively simple life. I found myself back in the "on" side of the relationship I'd turned off. The other guy was out, and she wanted to try again. I said there was no way. I didn't want anything to do with another attempt. I had effectively moved on. She pressured. I relented. I thought we might be able to work things out. I eventually learned that pressure and guilt are poor reasons to go back to a place you left long before.

I came back from Airborne school intent on trying to make things work in that relationship. I sensed that reconciling was a mistake, but I had to keep my word. I decided I could do this, and it was going to be good...or so I thought. It didn't take long before it was obvious- we were forcing things. Whatever magic we had before was gone. There was insecurity, questioning, tense exchanges...it just felt wrong. Before long, I knew it was over and we were on the outs again. Not totally out...but the beginning of the end. I distanced myself and just focused on work. I needed to just do what had to be done—end it definitively. Instead, I hoped it would just take care of itself. It did not.

After our introduction, things were quiet from 1LT Underwood. I was a little surprised by the silence, but I figured she was either busy, in a relationship, or waiting for me to make a move. I was too busy getting my life together to make a move. Besides, I had to finish cleaning up my mess before I pursued anyone. A few weeks after my return from Airborne school, I sat down and opened my email inbox to reveal a message from none other than...1LT Underwood!

What could this be? I wonder what she wants? Here we go!

The message opened something like... "Hello, LT Perry. I hope that you are doing well. We have formed a team to run the Army Ten-Miler. We need another person, and I was wondering if you would be willing to run with our team."

What?...the Army Ten-Miler?

Michael E. Perry

Well...that was not at all what I expected that email to say. I don't know exactly what I expected, but *the Army Ten-Miler*? I had intentionally avoided that run for years. Don't get me wrong, it is a fantastic event. I had gone to the staging and finishing areas before, but never participated. Ten miles of running for fun? Not interested. Of course, that was then. 1LT Wendy Underwood was asking me to run with her team. I responded with the only answer that made sense...
"Absolutely. I would love to run with your team. Leave me your telephone number so that I can follow up with you. By the way...you can call me "Mike."

Period. Send it.

The "dance" had begun. She sent her telephone number, and I waited for a few days without calling. I started feeling a little impatient...like I should call before she began to think I had no interest. Of course, I couldn't call too soon. After all, I had a reputation and a "vibe" to protect.

Can't seem desperate.
Can't seem disinterested.

It was a delicate balance. I thought it was time to check in, so I dialed up her phone. I would describe her outgoing message as "provocative." Her voice was all sexy and she basically challenged the caller to make it worth her time to listen. Well...this was a challenge I could not pass up. I hung up quickly before the tone sounded. I had to get set up properly for this...

Luther Vandross song playing in the background. Check.
Deep, sexy phone voice warmed up. Check.

Sitting in a real cool posture to ensure that my coolness conveyed through the phone. Check.

Time to redial. The machine picked up again, and I laid down some of the smoothest game ever to be laid down in 60 seconds or less. That's how I recall it, anyway.
It was officially "on" and I was going to bring my "A" game. Who knows what I actually said? All I know is that it had to be memorable for her.

Walter Reed was a magnet for VIPs—government and celebrity. My job included representing our General as an ambassador and guide, of sorts. It wasn't uncommon for me to be the first person to greet visitors as they entered the building. With Wendy working on the VIP ward, we collaborated on several occasions.

One such occasion was a major event hosted by the Commander's wife. Wendy led a team of nurses who were responsible for doing the lion's share of the work for the event. Headliners that week included track and field star and multiple Olympic gold medalist, Jackie Joyner-Kersee and U.S. Senator Bob Dole—a pretty big deal in 1997. I was tasked with keeping up with Bob Dole. I avoided a potentially embarrassing moment when someone told me to "make sure you shake his left hand." I thought I was being set up for a bad joke.

What? Why would I do that?

It was universally known that Bob Dole always carried a pen in his right hand. I knew that, but I did not know he was severely injured during World War II, rendering his right hand non-functional. He greeted people with his *left* hand. I discovered that detail only minutes before his arrival. Big oversight on my part. Embarrassing moment avoided.

Michael E. Perry

Wendy was responsible for Jackie Joyner-Kersee and her support team. We saw each other several times during the day, but we were professionals—completely focused on the job at hand. Ultimately, the event was an overwhelming success.

The Commander's wife was overjoyed on the next morning. She wanted me to let 1LT Underwood know how good a job she thought the nurses had done. In my opinion, there was no better time than the present to share that news...in person. Equipped with the only reason I needed to pay a visit to Wendy, I quickly made my way to the elevators. I went up to Ward 71 to find 1LT Underwood and share the great news. Approaching the Ward 71 entrance was like approaching the gates to the Land of Oz. The wood doors were massive—floor to ceiling—with no windows, and the passageways were monitored by closed circuit camera. I picked up the phone handset to request entry. Seconds later, one of the doors slowly opened, and I was greeted with a smile by one of the Soldiers working on the floor. He escorted me to the large station at the entrance to the ward. 1LT Underwood was standing there with her team.

"Mrs. K wanted me to pass on that you all did an amazing job. I thought I would come up and deliver that message personally." As I delivered that message, I was scanning the room and taking in data. I wanted to invite Wendy to lunch, but I didn't want to move too aggressively. Besides that, one of her friends—another nurse—was standing there, and I didn't want to seem dismissive. I had to do what I had to do to make this move, so I went for it..."Can I take you all to lunch to celebrate?"

At this point, the price of having a third wheel seemed worth the sacrifice if I was going to see if there was a real spark there between me and Wendy. At that moment, Wendy's friend demonstrated an act of grace and situational awareness that I will be eternally grateful for. She said, "Why don't you two go? I'll stay here!"

Thank you, Jesus!

"Ummm...are you sure?" I asked with great anticipation (and internal glee). She said yes, and Wendy asked for a few minutes to check off the floor. I went back to my office to report that I would be having lunch "with 1LT Underwood." That news was greeted with smiles and unanimous approval.

I was out the door and we were on the way to our first lunch together. The place...Woodside Deli on Georgia Avenue in Silver Spring, MD. The dish...open-faced turkey sandwiches. To date, that is the best turkey sandwich I have ever had. It was our first real conversation, and it was a great one. We talked about our families, our careers, likes, and dislikes. It seemed like lunch went on forever but was over too soon. By the time we were done on that Friday afternoon, the workday was just about over. I didn't want the day to end, and I figured she didn't either.

When I got back to work, it was almost time to leave for the day. I called her to ask, "How about a movie tonight?" I was on a roll. It was time to strike while the iron was red hot! "I already took the liberty of checking times, and I can pick you up," I said. She seemed more than happy to accept my invitation. I packed up and raced home to begin my pre-date ritual.

I called ahead to arrange tickets and got cleaned up. I was excited for this date in a way I had not been in a long time. I was also a little nervous. Was it possible to spend all afternoon with this woman and then go on a date on the same day? I got in my head a little...

Maybe I should just leave well-enough alone and give her a break... Nah...that's crazy.

It was a great first date. In fact, it seems like we were on a non-stop date for weeks following that day. That is, until non-stop...stopped.

It all seemed to be moving so fast. One night, a couple of weeks later, we went to dinner and a movie. I wanted to impress Wendy in every way. I even tied a cherry stem in a knot with my tongue. I don't know why...it just seemed like a good idea. Wendy was quite entertained.

I didn't want the date to end, and my sense was that Wendy felt the same way. We decided to take the 30-minute drive from Silver Spring to Downtown Washington, DC. First, we hit the National Mall, then Haynes Point Park. By this time in our short courtship, we were talking about everything...kids, finances, work, future, and God, among other things. Although the time was short, it seemed like Wendy was checking all the boxes and then some. Could she be "the one?" I was beginning to allow myself to imagine that she could.

We finished off that night at a place that became my favorite...the Jefferson Memorial. It was like we were the only two people on the planet that night. Just us...and Thomas Jefferson...looking over the placid Tidal Basin. We left D.C. and arrived at my apartment well after midnight and talked for several hours more.

Believe it or not, I had not yet made "my move." I figured it was time for a kiss, but I hesitated. I was normally more of a "swing for the fences" kind of guy, but my instincts were screaming that this one was different. I thought I might try a different approach..."Can I kiss you?" As that last word left my lips, I had a bit of a sinking feeling. Her response confirmed it..."No." My response... *"Why?"* "Because you asked." It's like my own thoughts screamed at me...

Aaaahhh. You played yourself, Mike!!!

You knew better than that! What were you thinking? Amateur move!

"Okay then. Next time," I said. Shortly after that moment, my cell began to ring. Then the house phone was next. The time must have been around 4 a.m. Multiple phones ringing at that time of the morning can mean only one thing...Drama. My "spidey senses" began to ping out of control. With many years of experience in how situations evolve from bad to worse, I knew there were two things to do. Silence that phone and get the heck out of that house. It was only a matter of time before there would be a knock on the door. The clock was ticking...

Time to go.

I said, "Okay, it's really late. Let's get you home." I later discovered that the knock did come. My college ace and roommate, Curt, was left to manage all that happened for the next several hours. He had a lot of explaining to do and emotion to manage on my behalf. He did that with little information and no idea when I would return. I still don't know that I've adequately repaid him for what he endured on that day.

Once I turned my phone back on, I was greeted by several voicemails—the first was from Curt, informing me that my estranged girlfriend had paid a visit to our apartment. The next several were messages from her, each revealing more distress than the last. First, the calls were from her home—then from my doorstep. For her, there was unfinished business. I was ready to end it. She was not.

When I returned home and learned she wanted a conversation to happen and would not take "no" for an answer, I knew that I had to tell Wendy about what was happening. Things were getting too intense, and I didn't want to drag her into any drama. I knew that this situation had the potential to derail everything, but I had no choice. Wendy had to know.

When I told Wendy that I had a relationship that was unresolved, she was understandably upset. That is when I first met the person I call "D.C. Wendy." Her message to me was fairly straightforward..."You need to handle your business and don't call me again until you do."

She was upset that there seemed to be so much going on, especially with a past love interest of mine knowing about Wendy, but with Wendy having no idea that such a person even existed. I could understand her point and her reasons for being upset.

At this point, I strongly sensed that Wendy was going to be the last woman I dated in my life, and I had already begun clearing all of the space in my life away for her. As my female "friends" checked in over time, I told them all that I met "the one" and would not be taking calls anymore. For the ones that did not call, I reached out to them to let them know. I was serious.

But there was one major loose end to tie up, and there was only one way out… "through." A sincere conversation with my estranged girlfriend was imminent. If this relationship was going to end, it would require time, effort, and honesty.

I made the phone call that day to fully own where I was and to call off things officially and finally. I did not fully grasp how difficult that task would be. There was a time when I would have buckled under the pressure that followed.

Our conversation began on a Sunday evening and did not end until the sun was rising on Monday morning. In past times, I would have been unable hold my position, given the level of pain I knew I was causing. I would have acquiesced and tried to give things another try. In the past, I likely would have made different decisions. On this day,

When: His Story.

however, that could not happen. Would not happen. There was one essential difference...Wendy.

I wanted to give Wendy something I had never given to any woman at that point. I wanted to truly give Wendy 100% of me—my attention, my commitment, and my life. It was early, but I was certain. Whatever the cost would be, it was worth it.

> *Psalm 37:23-24 (ESV)*
> *The steps of a man are established by the Lord, when he delights in his way; though he fall, he shall not be cast headlong, for the Lord upholds his hand.*

There was little else I was more certain of. After an agonizing day and night of negotiating, crying, arguing, defending, justifying, reliving, and simply standing—it was over.

A load lifted from my shoulders, but there was also a sense of sadness. At the outset of a relationship, emotional pain is never a feeling you anticipate will occur. Yet, here we were, and it was difficult. Doing what must be done can be hard on everyone. It was like an ultimate trial of my readiness to move to an entirely new place in my life and to be able to do that with Wendy.

After one of the most consequential weekends of my entire life, I went to work in a sleep-deprived state. I survived that day and then the next. When the time felt right, I called Wendy. It was time to see where life could take us. I was all in and completely swept away with this woman. I hadn't known this feeling before, but I knew it was right. I allowed myself to see an entire life with her. It felt completely right. I felt completely at peace.

Did you see anything you recognize?

The beginning of healing is just that…a start-point. Decisions and behavior can change instantly, but sometimes it takes life a while to catch up. There are no short cuts. I wanted something different for my life, but I had to do all of the work required to prepare myself and my space for the change. Have you started the work required to prepare yourself and your space for change?

When I Loved her.

I think I loved Wendy from the day we sat down over open-faced turkey sandwiches. After nearly destroying our relationship before it began, I felt a level of emptiness that I'd not experienced before. We were not speaking. The fact that we had been connecting for only a period of weeks made things feel more extreme. I did not care. I needed to find out if this was real or not, and I was going to do whatever it took to do that. I was willing to look like a fool for the small chance that this was the relationship that I never even dared to dream about.

I contacted Wendy to ask if we could meet. I wanted to assure her that she had nothing to worry about. I made it clear that I wanted to see where things could go with us. For the first time, I had a singular focus, and Wendy was it. Our relationship accelerated rapidly after that. I was still in a very demanding job, but everywhere we looked, people were helping our relationship along. We began eating breakfast and lunch together every day. Sometimes those moments would go a little long. My boss seemed to be unphased. Wendy's boss seemed not to care much. It's almost like they were clearing the way for us. On an official trip or two, Wendy came along, and we would just sightsee and enjoy each other's company (during my downtime, of course).

There was one event that I believe showed Wendy I cared for her and was willing to drop everything to be there for her if necessary. I invited her on a special date. By "special" I mean an epic date to end all dates. The Zachary and Elizabeth Fisher Foundation had been building "Fisher Houses" on military bases all over the country to provide care-free living spaces for family members supporting service members undergoing surgical care. Walter Reed was about to dedicate their second Fisher House on a date that coincided with Zachary Fisher's 87th birthday in 1997. Representatives from the foundation would be onsite at Walter Reed for the festivities. Mr. Fisher wanted to attend but could not because his health limited his ability to travel. That was the bad news. The good news was that he scheduled a party near his home—in New York City—and he invited about 200 people from Walter Reed to attend...in New York. On the same day as the dedication. Chartered flight, escorted buses, gala event, multi-course menu, open bar...all arranged by the Fishers!

I asked Wendy if she would attend the event with me. We only had a day to plan, so she was off to her hairdresser the next afternoon—only hours before we were to take the ride to Andrews Air Force Base to board the charter flight bound for New York City. I received an early afternoon phone call. It was Wendy, and something was wrong. She had been in a car accident, and she needed my help. In a matter of seconds, I closed out everything I was doing and went out to find her. When I arrived on the scene, her car was being hauled away, but she was not there. Where did I find her? After the scene was processed, Wendy wasted no time. SHE KEPT HER APPOINTMENT and WALKED THE REMAINING HALF BLOCK to her hairdresser! I was relieved to see her after that accident and stayed with her until she was done. I was concerned that she might be injured, but she was concerned about getting ready for the event. She said her body was sore, but that was not going to stop her from getting on that plane. That is exactly what she did.

The evening was magical. It was a once-in-a-lifetime experience. The charter 747 flight to Newark airport would have been more than enough under normal circumstances, but these were not normal circumstances. We landed and immediately hopped on luxury buses. Those buses formed a convoy that was escorted north on I-95 toward Manhattan by a police motorcade, blocking off the highway and stopping southbound traffic at the Lincoln tunnel so that we could travel through, against the flow of traffic, with no delay. The time was around 6pm. That's right... We traveled up I-95 during rush hour in New York City with all vehicular traffic blocked from the highway and then went northbound through a southbound tunnel into Manhattan! I did not know that Zachary Fisher had that kind of pull. He clearly did. Upon arrival in Manhattan, it was off the buses and onto the Intrepid—a re-purposed World War II era aircraft carrier- turned-museum—for an extravagant gala affair. As amazing as that date was, it was the fact that we were doing it together that seemed to be most special. We were back on our plane and landing in Maryland just around midnight. After our return to Walter Reed, we stopped at the emergency room to have Wendy checked out. She *was* in a car accident after all. The first of countless magical moments to come was complete.

With a major jumpstart to our relationship, we were soon off to another major milestone—taking Wendy home to meet my family for the first time at a large event—a Halloween party. We left work and immediately jumped on the road, getting into costume on the way. Wendy was a black cat. I knew she was a gifted artist, but I was stunned at how she was able to use a few basic materials to turn herself into a sexy, classy, black cat on the way down I-95. Four hours later and we were there. The family was taken with her. I was too.

I had recently met Wendy's father in Baltimore. Prior to the visit, I was clueless about what to expect. My charm typically went a long way with people. Something told me that Wendy's father would not be easily charmed. I figured he would be different. Was he ever?

Wendy's father was stricken with what was thought to be ALS, also known as Lou Gehrig's Disease, which rendered him unable to use his lower extremities and left arm. Despite his condition, Gary Underwood made the most of what he had and never complained. During our initial meeting, he laid silently in his bed. He then pushed the button to slowly tilt the head of his bed upward. After what seemed like an agonizingly long wait, he released the button, stopping the bed. He made eye contact with me and asked something like...

"What the hell do you think you're doing with my daughter?"

Then he calmly pushed the "down" button and awaited my response. I don't recall what I said. I only remember going through about 2 more cycles of that process before he let me off the hook! Wendy's dad was hilarious and real. He accepted me instantly. I believe that he accepted me because he wanted whatever made Wendy happy...and she was happy.

At the point Wendy met my family, it was already pretty much a wrap for me. I wasn't looking for approval or agreement. She was the one. I visited her apartment one day at a time...for countless consecutive days. She tends to say we were "shackin'." I never took a key to her place, so I like to think I was "visiting" daily with occasional breaks to check on my apartment and my roommate.

Don't judge me. You've got your own lies you tell yourself.

I would like my truth to be that we established our relationship by the book and saved our sexual relationship for marriage. That is not my truth. We knew that sex before marriage can complicate things and cloud judgement. We also knew that our sexual relationship was counter to God's will for marriage. The problem in those moments was that it didn't *feel* complicated or wrong. It seemed crystal clear.

In fact, it seemed more simple, organic, real, and right than anything. That was my truth.

We entered a period of time that seemed too magical to be true. For the first time, I felt like there was nothing else to search for. Until then, there had been a constant press—what I would describe as tension. Never fully settled and always looking, or at least, open to the next possibility. Suddenly, all other possibilities evaporated. Wendy was enough. Everyone seemed to be cheering for us and encouraging our growing relationship.

One great example was the day we sat down with General Benjamin O. Davis, Jr. and his wife, Agatha, as they visited Walter Reed. Yes...*that* Benjamin O. Davis—commander of the Tuskegee Airmen. I don't have words sufficient to describe what that conversation meant. They were kind and down-to-earth, and they shared a lifetime of experience in mere minutes. The coolest part was how they encouraged us and validated the love growing between us. At that point, they had been married for about 60 years! They were very sweet together, and they gave us a glimpse of what our future could be.

I wanted that future, so I continued to clean up my life. I thought it was time to completely empty my address book in my quest to give Wendy 100% of my attention. She was all I could see.

To allow yourself to fall deeply into love with another person requires a level of vulnerability that feels risky. I was there. Fully vulnerable but feeling no risk. I had burned all my previous bridges. I took all my eggs, and they were in one basket. I was all in. It was time to say those three words. I didn't even think twice about it. We were sitting together one evening, maybe after a meal. I looked her right into her eyes and said it..."I love you."

A moment of silence passed. Just as we were spiraling from silent to awkward, she gave a nod...ever so slight...and at the same time said..."Okay."

Okay??? What the hell just happened???

I was disoriented for a moment. Then, I went into my head big time.

Damn. You just played yourself, Mike...again. Maybe she played you. You have been on the wrong side of this type of exchange enough times to know that you just keep your damn mouth shut.
You got caught up.

Did you get it wrong? Did you push her? Are you giving up everything for someone who is not in the same place?

This is where a little of the simplicity disappeared. I knew Wendy's history. She was engaged before and it ended suddenly. She had dealt with hurt in the past. She had dealt with uncommitted men in the past. She'd lost her mother relatively recently. I knew all that. Somehow, when I put it out there with those three small words, it became about me and my risk, not hers.

To add to that, the perfect world we'd built was tested from time-to-time by the ghosts of relationships past. Ours is a good example of how a sexual relationship and live-in situation complicate matters a bit, especially around matters of the heart. Wendy's phone would ring, and she would not answer, or she would tell me to answer it. When I acquiesced and answered, there would be silence. If she answered, there was always a response. I thought that those conversations should be swift and merciless. In my imagination, I scripted them something like this...

Thanks for calling and never call again. We are over and my new man is standing right here. Get lost!

When: His Story.

That's what I wanted to hear. I was so well-versed at how "the dance" goes when a man is trying to talk that talk, I could fill in the blanks and determine what her caller was saying by Wendy's words, tones, or silence. I considered walking out. I did not. I didn't like it, but I knew I had to give her a chance to work things out on her terms in her way. After all, her choice was clear. That choice was me. I wasn't going anywhere, even if it required a battle or two. I was down for that. I loved her. I was 100% sold out.

We endured the turbulence of past relationships and continued to create these amazing moments crafted with simple ingredients. It seems people were still trying to help us all along the way. For example, Wendy wanted crabs one night, so I ventured out to the only spot still open—a mobile crab joint about 5 minutes away. I was the last customer of the night and he threw in a few extra. I grabbed Wendy's favorite beer at the time, Miller Genuine Draft Light (MGD), and headed back. As we ate, drank, and laughed on her balcony that night, those crabs seemed like the best we'd ever had.

We traveled to local attractions we had overlooked in the past. Solomon's Island, Maryland was a great one. It was simple and amazing. We purchased our first live Christmas tree together that weekend, because Wendy wanted a tree. That's all it took. I was driving my Toyota Camry. It was white, and it was clean. It had gotten me safely to and from Texas, and it had taken me thousands of miles elsewhere. I loved that car, and every Saturday morning I took the time to restore it to its original splendor. I did not believe in stickers, magnets, or anything that might leave even the slightest blemish on that vehicle. The single exception? A medium sized red bow that I had attached to the emblem in the grille on the front of the car during the holidays. It was simple, and I thought it was classy without being too much. Now, Wendy wanted a Christmas tree.

Wendy eyed her perfect tree, and since we were at least two hours from home, there was no option to run back and find one of my friends with a truck to pick this thing up. I did what I would have considered unthinkable only weeks before. I strapped that tree across the trunk of my beloved Camry. At that moment, the Camry became *just a car*. Wendy's happiness and joy were more important than any scratch or scuff on a material item, even with as much care as I had put into that item. That moment might have revealed a turning point for me. We ended up driving to Potomac Mills, in Woodbridge, VA and all-over Northern Virginia, D.C., and Maryland with that tree strapped to my car. Hundreds of miles in the course of a day. We returned to Wendy's place and decorated that tree like a couple of pros. One of the best days ever, ended with one of the most beautiful first-time trees I'd seen. It seemed like everything we experienced was just more...More beautiful. More memorable. More satisfying.

During my "purge" season only a couple of months earlier, I eliminated almost all female contacts from my life, except one. We tried to maintain a friendship, despite past intimacy, discussing family, future, politics...things that friends discuss. That lasted for a while but could not last forever.

She liked nice things—often expensive things—and would occasionally give nice gifts. She didn't overdo it, but she did step it up with gifts on special occasions. As it happens, my birthday was approaching, and she sent me a watch—a really nice time piece that was quite expensive. I didn't tell Wendy about it, because I believed that the watch would only create drama and perhaps a little suspicion.

Wendy was accepting, but she was also initially a bit skeptical about my friendship with this woman. It was interesting that Wendy didn't make demands, behave jealously, or pressure me in any way to dissolve my friendship. Still, when the watch arrived, I just held on to it for a few days, pondering what to do. Keep it, wear it, and risk drama? Keep it and hide it to avoid drama? Send it back and hurt feelings but avoid drama? I decided it was better to send it back. I couldn't keep secrets from Wendy, so keeping the watch and just not mentioning it seemed a poor choice. I guessed Wendy would understand and even celebrate my decision. I figured my friend would understand that I was trying to build something that I did not want to jeopardize, and one returned watch was a small price to pay for that cause. I was wrong on both fronts. My friend did not understand and was not pleased. Wendy was straight-up pissed. She was angry that I didn't mention it and angry I sent it back. I just couldn't win.

And so, began our first major blow-out as a couple. I was expecting appreciation and congratulations. I got questions and frustration. Sure, I had held on to a few pieces of vital information, but I eventually came around. To Wendy, it was almost a replay of the events at the beginning of our courtship. Things were happening around her and she didn't know, and she didn't like it. First, we argued. Then, we shut down. Before long, she was on the phone with her best friend or sister—I was never certain. Whoever it was, she was ranting like I hadn't seen. She even drank a couple of MY beers while she did it. I was hot. I wanted to leave but decided to stay in place for the moment. She went to bed without a word. I was still reeling, trying to figure out what had just happened. At first, I was focused on the issue...

Why was giving that watch back such a big deal?

Then, the nature of the questions I asked myself began to shift...

What are you doing here anyway?

Why are you even trying this hard?

You don't have to deal with any of this.

I thought long into the night. The questions shifted again...

Do you love her? Absolutely yes.

Can you see yourself with anyone else? Absolutely, not.

Can you see spending the rest of your life with her? Without question.

Well then...what are you waiting for? She is the one you prayed for...

That moment shook me.

All of my anger had given way to clarity. Wendy was my wife. I knew it more than anything I'd known. I had no plan, no money, and no ring. All I knew was that Wendy was the wife that I prayed for. I was damaged goods and did not deserve her. But I also realized that I could give her something I had given to no one else—my entire life and my total heart. It couldn't wait. I had to ask her to marry me...immediately. The time was about 2:00 a.m.

The radio was on, and I wanted to wait for the right song, so I waited.

> *1 John 5:14-15 (ESV)*
> *And this is the confidence that we have toward him, that if we ask anything according to his will he hears us. And if we know that he hears us in whatever we ask, we know that we have the requests that we have asked of him..*

When: His Story.

About six songs played…all garbage. I was getting desperate. Given that we were about 10 years pre-music streaming services, my options were limited to over-the-air radio, compact discs, and cassettes. I had nothing ready to go, so I was relying on the radio station. They were failing me at this point. And then, a small glimmer of light— "Just to be Close to You" by Lionel Ritchie and the Commodores. Not necessarily what I would have picked, but the gamble was too risky to wait for the next song.

    I moved in close and gently touched her to wake her up. No prepared speech. No ring. No crowd. Just us. I let her know what I had realized in the hours before. I believed that she was the one chosen for me. She was my wife. Despite anything that attempted to stand in our way, I had no desire to be with anyone else and I only wanted to spend the rest of my life with her at my side. I promised her that I would make every year better than the last. And I meant it…

"Will you marry me?"

    She needed time to get her bearings. I'm sure that this conversation was the last thing she expected when she stormed to the room and went to sleep. We had dated for barely six months. She said, "yes." There in the darkness and silence of her apartment, we hugged and wept.

Did you see anything you recognize?

What is influencing your actions and decision making? Is there any such thing as waiting too long or moving too quickly to get married to the one you love? How often are your decisions driven by people and circumstances outside of yourself or your relationship? Who determines when the time is right for you? If there are more than two people in your decision-making process, there might be too many.

When I Married her.

I had no idea how to be a married man. But I knew that Wendy was the one, and we would figure the rest out like everyone else had before us. I also knew that my marriage would be different than what I'd seen growing up. We were going to make it, and divorce and drama were not options.

It seemed fast, and in some ways, it was. From first date to proposal was 6 or 7 months—much quicker than the way I imagined my engagement would happen. Wendy and I decided on a wedding date of April 4th. That meant that from our first meeting to our wedding would be just under a year. The speed of that timeline was shocking to more than a few people. How could I—given my "reputation"—be among the first of my friends to get married? Had enough time passed for me to know for sure? That's what many people asked. A close neighborhood friend asked, "Can't love wait?" My response was swift. "No, it cannot. When you know, you know." I knew.

When we announced our engagement, there was mostly celebration around us. It was like everyone could feel what we felt. They were on our side and pulling for us. Wendy and I had already received military orders for one-year assignments to Korea that same year. As we saw it, we had two choices: get married before we left or wait until we returned, over a year later. There was only one choice as we saw it—we had to get this wedding done before we left for the Korean peninsula. That meant an accelerated planning process, so we had to get started.

As it turns out, Wendy had placed a deposit on a reception space for the wedding she had planned before her previous engagement fell through. The idea of using funds from previous marriage plans didn't set well with me initially. As far as I was concerned, those funds, used or unused, were attached to a past situation that I believed should remain out of site and out of mind. The problem with that? We were not rich, and we were committed to funding our own wedding. It wasn't feasible to essentially throw away thousands of dollars. I had to get over myself and see this for what it was—a blessing in the form of a down payment on Wendy's real wedding...to me. I put my pride aside, and we started to plan. Only a few months later it was time. I was ready.

Along the way, tragedy struck. My grandfather—my dad's father—passed away about a week before our wedding. I knew he was ill, but I didn't prepare myself for him to die. Our family had been blessed with an extended season of relatively good health and longevity. My only experiences with death and loss were at a distance. In a way, I felt guilty for the pain I felt. Wendy lost her mother only a couple of years prior, and it seemed like her family had to endure so much more loss than my family did. She always seemed so steady and strong. I don't think I fully appreciated what must have been happening with her under the surface.

I had to take time to mourn and honor my grandfather, but with some discussion and prayer, we decided to continue moving our wedding plans forward. I traveled to North Carolina for the funeral. I felt connected to my grandfather in a special way. He had his problems, but I saw him as a peaceful and kind man who always seemed to project goodness. We visited him frequently growing up. Whether it was getting an orange soda from the "juke joint" (that's what we called it) he ran next door when we were young, watching him summon his chickens, throwing my football around, or just sitting for hours on his porch, my grandfather was a solid fixture in our lives and a great influence on mine.

I know he had deep pain that we never knew about. On occasion, my dad would get a call that my grandfather had been drinking *again*. Dad would drive down and often find granddaddy in the street. He would bring him to our home and clean him up. I didn't know what pain he was attempting to ease with alcohol, but I knew I didn't want to be that way. But his goodness—I could use that, so I kept it. I pinned a set of my Airborne wings on his lapel at his funeral. I went back home, found Wendy, and just let go and wept. I needed her, and she was there.

The morning of our wedding the following week was cloudy with a light drizzle. Some say that rain on your wedding day means good luck, fertility, a long marriage, etc. I didn't need superstition on this day. I was beyond certain. The night before, I called an early end to my bachelor activities. A couple of the fellas were probably close to being arrested anyway. Wendy was with her bridesmaids and friends. It was one of the few nights I had not seen her, and I was ready to get this ceremony going.

We were married at the Walter Reed Chapel. On that day I arrived at the chapel several hours early. It felt majestic, yet simple. Grand, but intimate. I just stood at the entrance and envisioned what the room would look like in a few hours. Some people get nervous prior to their wedding, but I was at total peace. I was...eager. I can't recall a time when I was so certain even when the stakes were so high.

Curt was my best man, and he met me at the chapel early that morning. We prayed in a back room before people started to arrive. It was a special moment. There are few people that see us at our worst and best in the same lifetime. There are fewer still who are just steady and always there if you need them. Curt had been that for me for years. It was the kind of friendship that stays on "simmer" so-to-speak. It didn't need to be proven or affirmed. It just was. There was no competition (well...not much). It's the type of friendship every man needs.

After that prayer, I was focused, and time moved quickly. As the organizers and participants began to arrive, I became more and more eager. It was time to get dressed.

I chose a rarely seen Army uniform...Mess Whites. I selected it because it was different, and it looked like something a young prince might wear.

The most noticeable element of the uniform was the waist-length white jacket with gold buttons and trim. Most people had never seen this uniform and would not recognize it as Army attire. I knew that it was the only uniform worthy of marking this moment in time. It was expensive, but Wendy was well worth it. Besides, she liked to see me in those pants!

By the time I was dressed, the two pastors charged with officiating the wedding had arrived. Yep...two. Our entire wedding was a family affair, and we created special and unique opportunities for family members to participate. Our wedding was officiated by my Uncle, mom's eldest brother, and my lifelong next-door neighbor, a church pastor. They both played special roles in my life growing up. My uncle was the lead officiant, and his most important role was to bring it home with the vows.

Our organist was a decades-long friend of my parents and former organist at my childhood church. He basically adopted me, my sisters, and cousins. He also happened to live in the Washington, D.C. area and pastored a church downtown. We asked my mom and one of my aunts to each sing a song. My father and Wendy's father teamed up to give her away. My dad was to walk Wendy down the aisle and present her to her father. Wendy's father was to complete the journey in his motorized wheelchair and give her away.

The wedding party was stacked with family and close friends from home, college, and work. As everyone trickled in on that cloudy morning, I was happy to see them, but it

When: His Story.

Michael E. Perry

was as if I was looking right through them all. I was ready to see my wife walk through those doors.

After ensuring our music was set and ready, I got word that Wendy had arrived. It was time.

Over 200 people packed into the Walter Reed Chapel for our wedding. The pastors positioned themselves front and center, and Curt and I joined them shortly after. My heart was beating out of my chest as the organ began to play. I was completely calm and completely elated as the ceremony began. As the bridesmaids and groomsmen entered, I felt a sense of... triumph. Each of those men who stood for me that day had been on the journey in some way. The good and bad. The victory and defeat. On this day, they walked down that aisle looking like a group of champions. My victory was theirs, and it felt amazing, and then, the moment of truth...

The organ stopped, and the door cracked open. Wendy was not visible yet. Suddenly, over 20 late guests scurried through the crack in the door and scrambled to find seats! It was standing room only at that point. I noticed them, but I barely saw them. The doors closed, and a song began to play. It was a song we'd chosen specially for Wendy's entrance—"Whenever You Call," performed by Mariah Carey. From the first time we heard this song, it was going to be played at our wedding...

"Love wandered inside
stronger than you, stronger than I,
and now that it has begun,
we cannot turn back
we can only turn into one.
I won't ever be too far away to feel you,
and I won't hesitate at all
whenever you call.
And I'll always remember,
the part of you so tender,

When: His Story.

*I'll be the one to catch your fall,
Whenever you call..."*

As the song began, the doors were pulled open, and she was there. Her veil was down, but I could see her face. She looked nervous, but ready. She seemed more beautiful than I had ever seen her. My dad stood there as tall as a soldier. He was ready for the moment. Once they began to move down the aisle, I had tunnel vision. All I could see was Wendy's face. That was it.

When they reached Wendy's father, he maneuvered his chair into place with an impressive level of precision. He knew Wendy was concerned that her wedding gown might be pulled into the wheels on his chair. There was no chance of that happening on this day.

At the instant Wendy's father gave her away, I felt the responsibility that was passed. I gladly accepted everything that moment meant. I would honor her, cherish her, love her, and protect her with every ounce of my being. I wanted her father to know

> *Genesis 2:23 (ESV)*
> *Then the man said, "This at last is bone of my bones and flesh of my flesh; she shall be called Woman, because she was taken out of Man.*

that he didn't have to worry. I think he felt that.

The ceremony seemed to race by. Before I knew it, it was time for the rings and the vows. Just as a precautionary measure, we chose not to include the part about anyone having "any reason this couple should not be married, blah, blah…" No need to invite any surprises!

After we exchanged rings, we prayed, and it was time for the kiss. When I heard those words… "You may now salute your bride," well…I did. Let's just say we kissed like we had actually kissed before. Sometimes couples kiss at

Michael E. Perry

their weddings like they are afraid that their parents may disapprove or something. Wendy and I were not hampered by any such hang ups! It was done. And it was amazing. I was now looking into the eyes of my wife.

We had about a month to prepare for our upcoming move to Korea. We knew that our assignments were supposed to be in different areas, but we were unsure of how everything would work. This was our first military assignment overseas and only the second in both our young careers. Saying goodbye to family was always difficult for me, but on this trip, the sting was reduced because Wendy and I were together.

Arriving in Korea and walking into Kimpo International Airport was like walking into another universe. I kept imagining what it might be like to experience something like this alone, and I was grateful that we could experience it together. We retrieved our bags, found a taxi, and made our way to the Dragon Hill Lodge, an impressive hotel that many people might be shocked to find on a military base. We arrived just in time to celebrate Wendy's birthday, and the Dragon Hill was the perfect backdrop. Dinner...flowers...it was like we were on an exotic vacation.

But this was no vacation. We were in country on a mission, with only a couple of days to prepare ourselves for the challenges we faced. We arrived believing we would be in separate parts of the country, but when we checked in, they said that I would be assigned to a unit near Seoul, which would allow me to live with Wendy. That was not what we planned, but we were certainly happy to hear it. We had not been looking forward to being separated and living in different cities, especially after being recently married and moving to a foreign country. We were relieved, but that relief was short-lived.

The next day, we learned that the original plan was the correct plan—I was set to report to a base close to the

When: His Story.

De-militarized Zone (DMZ) on the Korean peninsula—Camp Casey. For a moment, we had allowed ourselves to believe we would live in Seoul together, so the truth was a difficult pill to swallow. I packed up and prepared to board the bus to head north to Camp Casey. For the previous 9 months, Wendy and I were together almost daily. Saying goodbye and getting on that bus was difficult. We were in the same country, but it felt like we were worlds apart. I remember watching couples walk together as the bus traveled through the city streets. It always seems like everyone else is really happy in moments when you are really low. It definitely seemed that way as I made my way to my unit. I would experience that feeling many times over the course of the year.

I was the platoon leader of the medical platoon in an armor (tank) battalion. Although my heart wanted to be elsewhere, I went about the business of learning my new job and getting to know my new Soldiers. By that point, I had learned valuable lessons about how to push through tough times until the adjustment happened. That was made easier in Korea, because there was so much to learn in such a short time.

In my new unit, our job was to be on alert and ready to go to war within just hours. That meant periodic drills requiring me to have my platoon loaded up and ready to roll out at any point. The challenge for me was the practice I developed of leaving work on Friday afternoons and getting down to Seoul as fast as I could—about 2 hours, on average, by train. The bus was a slightly shorter ride, but the scheduling was not as convenient.

If an alert came, public transit could not get be back fast enough to meet my required response time. I resolved that issue with a very friendly taxi driver I met—we'll call him Sam. He was based in Seoul and I told him that there may be times when I needed to get back to Camp Casey in a hurry. Sam assured me he could get me back in less than

Michael E. Perry

an hour and a half. I kept his card in my wallet for the entire year, although I never had to use it.

When I could, I spent my weekends—Friday to Sunday evening—with Wendy. Assignment to Camp Casey meant that we needed a pass from our commander to leave our base and visit other parts of the Korean peninsula. There were times when I had a pass and times when I just went rogue. Those rogue days were funny, because I was with other people on the bus and train—some that I worked for and some who worked for me—who didn't have passes either. Sometimes it's just best to agree to keep things quiet. No words required.

Wendy lived in a quaint 2-bedroom, second floor apartment in a neighborhood about 10 minutes outside of the base at Yongsan. Her landlord lived in the unit below, and she could see me coming from a block away. She always announced my arrival to Wendy. The funny thing is that this woman could not speak a word of English, but she and Wendy seemed to communicate perfectly. That was always a gift of Wendy's that amazed me and drew me closer to her. She was—and still is—able to get immediately beneath the surface and really "see" people—who they are, how they feel, and what they mean. It is remarkable to watch. I still feel a little sheepish when I turn to her and say, "What did they say?"

I lived for those Fridays when I could wrap things up, run to the train or bus station, and make the 2-hour trek to see my bride. It was like a reunion every time. I was whole again. During the week, I was 100% leader of my platoon and special advisor to the command team at the battalion. When I got to Wendy, I was just a man who wanted to hold his wife. We spent our time shopping, seeing the city, and traveling. We also celebrated holidays, American and Korean.

Less than two months in, we bought a dog—a little white Bichon. He was for sale with other puppies on the street in a popular market across town. That move was impulsive, but this was one cute dog. The look on Wendy's face made the choice a simple one. We would have to figure it out. "Kimpo" was about to get a new home. Wendy had decided to leave her cat, Simba, in the states to avoid distressing him with overseas travel and quarantine requirements. She was lonely, so Kimpo was the right addition to our new family at the right time.

As we were approaching the halfway point of our year in Korea, tragedy was about to strike…again. My cousin was diagnosed with cervical cancer before we left, and although she was receiving treatment, she was not getting better. In October, I received a call from home. The end was near. I contacted Wendy, and we arranged to get a flight as fast as we could. That was not an easy task, but our commanders did their part to get us approved. When we checked in at the airport, our flight was delayed without explanation. After a couple of hours, the flight was cancelled until the next day. There was nothing we could do. My cousin passed while we were in the air on the next day. I was devastated and angry at the airline. The truth is, there was nothing anyone could have done. That was difficult to acknowledge, but it was a valuable lesson in acceptance and letting go. It would be a lesson I would learn many times over…and benefit from as well.

We returned to Korea and discovered that Wendy was pregnant! We frequently discussed how we would plan babies into our lives and careers, and we believed the timing was just about right. We were wrong. Wendy miscarried. When she called to deliver the news, I was in shock—this was the last thing I expected. I made my way to Yongsan as soon as I could that night. I was hurting, but I knew that Wendy's pain was more than I could imagine. Sometimes there is nothing to say when terrible things happen. I had no adequate words for that moment—only my presence. It was another serious punch in the gut for our young relationship. I had the sense that we could overcome it together, but I also had the sense that Wendy took that on herself as a personal failure. It's easy to tell someone "it's not your fault," but it can be difficult for the recipient to accept those words.

Even during tragedy and difficult times, there are often good times and great memories. We visited Thailand, Hong Kong, and Singapore and experienced things together that revealed we were more alike than we knew from the beginning. In Bangkok, we decided to take a ride on a Tuk-Tuk one morning. A Tuk-Tuk is a three-wheeled motorcycle with covered seating for two passengers on the back. Off we went, careening down the streets of Bangkok in some of the gnarliest traffic you will ever experience. The driver was...well...aggressive. I'm pretty sure we were close to death at least 3 times that we knew of. After we arrived at our destination, all we could do was laugh uncontrollably. That event helped us appreciate the value of sharing a terrifying experience with the one you love and living to tell the story. It was also evidence that we probably needed adult supervision because it was apparent neither one of us knew where to draw the line on our adventures! We would have many more of those experiences in the years that followed.

During the second half of our Korea assignment, Wendy's father's health took a turn for the worse. It was so bad, in fact, that we were granted an unprecedented second trip back home to the U.S. When we arrived, he was not responding to anyone—not even Wendy. I was really concerned for her. How could she lose her father after having lost her mother not long before? How would she be able to endure that? I just tried to stand and be stable and steady for her.

We had only a few days in town before we were required to return to Korea, and nothing changed until we were preparing to leave. He was responding, but he was uncharacteristically harsh and silent. It seemed like he was pushing away the people he loved. On the day of our last visit, Wendy had a very straight forward, one-way conversation with her father, basically telling him that she was going to have to return to Korea. She also told him that he was going to have to fight for himself if he wanted to live, because she could not do it for him. She looked him straight in the eyes and told him she loved him and gave him permission to make his choice. After she helped clean him up, we left. I was not certain we would see him again.

Shortly after we returned to Korea, we learned that Gary was making his way back. He soon returned to his normal pleasant, trash-talking, no-nonsense personality. An enormous weight had been lifted for Wendy, because leaving her father as he was felt to me like we were saying goodbye, but Gary Underwood was not done living yet! It was another reminder that nothing is guaranteed—each moment carries with it an opportunity to choose life or to wait for death.

They say plans are made to be broken, and after a challenging year, we decided to shatter our plans. In that time, we learned that although we placed great value on planning, timing, and precision, life didn't care much about our plans. We both believed that family was paramount, so we decided to let the family come as it might, and we would plan around that. No plan. Just do it and work out the rest. Before we left Korea, we succeeded. Baby #1 was on the way.

Did you see anything you recognize?

The early years of a marriage can feel like a roller coaster ride or a rocket ship. Our experience was a bit of both. Blending two lives into one is a challenge, and with each added variable the challenge grows more complicated. I often wonder if the volatility in our first year eclipsed other seemingly insignificant issues that we might have addressed under normal circumstances. Some of those issues were hidden…waiting to emerge when the dust settled. Is there anything waiting for you?

When I Hurt her.

When we returned to the United States, we set out to begin building our "normal" life together for the first time. We got a new SUV and towed my car—the one we'd kept at my father's house—down to San Antonio. First order of business—buy a house and furniture. Before long, our home was taking shape. Wendy loved to arrange and decorate. She was really good at it too. After the major areas of the house were taken care of, our attention turned to the baby's room. I cannot recall the total number of visits we made to the Baby Depot, but there were many!

In December 1999, our first daughter was born, almost a year after our miscarriage. It was a tough delivery—Wendy spent about 24 hours in labor. Despite a grueling process that included the dreaded "spinal headache" and an ultimate determination that she would have to undergo a C-section, Wendy was a superhero. When it was all done, the entire world seemed to have shifted in one moment. We created another life, and we were responsible to help develop who this person would be in the world. It was overwhelming. I immediately saw Wendy in this baby's face. That moment defies description.

Wendy decided months before that she would breastfeed, which meant that the baby would encroach on pretty-much all of the space and time that had previously been mine. Although there were times when I wanted my wife back, I was content to allow the process of bonding and nurturing to occur without becoming jealous and impatient. This was a complete team effort. Wendy began to say that I was like her "Superman" and gave me a gift or two with that iconic logo.

Our lives were busy before the baby, but when Wendy returned to work, the challenges felt exponential. There was another human being to account for, and there would be no neglect or shortcomings where she was concerned. As we continued to build our young careers, there was also pressure to consistently show up and be at our best at work. I sometimes worked irregular or overnight hours, and Wendy was frequently assigned the night shift. This made getting the baby to and from daycare a real challenge with little room for error. Despite the stressors of a growing family, we were handling things well. Our marriage still felt as perfect as it did on the day we took our vows. Still, the growing list of things we were required to attend to, at home and work, made some of the routine things at home a bit of a strain.

By far, the top issue we faced was who would cook meals at dinner time. Way back when we were dating, it was no secret that I enjoyed cooking—the process and the outcome. Wendy was not as motivated by the process. Cooking was more of a pragmatic function for her...get fed. However that happened, Wendy was cool with it. In our discussions prior to Korea, she talked about how she would begin cooking after we were married and moved into a home together. In Korea, we agreed that most of our time be spent enjoying each other and creating experiences. At that point, the conversations were about what life would look like when we were back in the U.S. and raising a family. She said she would cook more when we settled down in the states.

As life began to take shape in San Antonio, it was clear that the "new normal" around our process for meals was not taking hold. The typical conversation went something like this...

"What are we doing for dinner tonight?"
"I don't know. What do you want?
"I don't know. Do you know what you want?"

When: His Story.

"Not really..."

The rest is probably predictable. After a bit of back-and-forth, we might go and grab something, sit down at a restaurant, or put something together there at the house. If there was going to be a meal prepared at home, I was the one who was most likely to prepare it. I became a little annoyed and then frustrated with that. I recounted the conversations about "when we get back" to create a "normal" life. Over time, I interpreted Wendy's aspirations about cooking as "promises" to be kept, and I formed a set of expectations around those promises. I became increasingly vocal, and tension between us slowly increased.

After the events of 9-11, we decided that we were going to try for a second child, and just like that, our second daughter was on the way. At this point, we were in the phase of our military careers where each subsequent job was going to stress our ability to manage time, take care of our family, and continue to grow closer together as a couple. At times, it seemed like we only saw each other in parking lots to swap the babies, or for a few hours at home before it was time for one of us to leave. It was a time when I often thought about whether it was worth it to continue serving in the military, but we were both in the emerging stages of our careers and getting out of the military seemed to leave too much possibility on the table.

Our capacity for handling those routine household tasks was also being stretched. I began commenting with increasing regularity about Wendy's cooking frequency or lack thereof. First to Wendy, then to others—mostly family members of mine. It became somewhat of a running narrative...Wendy's cooking. Others were feeling totally comfortable inquiring with Wendy as to whether or not she had cooked lately. I created the space for conversations that were not uplifting or encouraging for her. As a result, the ongoing frustration began to erode the fortress walls we had erected together. There was more tension and strained communication between us than there had been at any point in our relationship. It didn't feel like we were in trouble, but we clearly had some threats to our paradise that we did not recognize. I certainly didn't. With a second child now in the picture, the pressure only increased.

There were behaviors I allowed to enter our space that slowly weakened the defenses I had erected when we met. I always protected Wendy from anyone who might speak anything negative toward her. With those conversations about cooking, I was not protecting her. I also made it my habit to ensure that I discussed Wendy with everyone I met, especially other women. It was important to me that everyone knew that I was completely off the market and not shopping for anything! I did a great job at that in the beginning, but I was employing my "Wendy shield" with less frequency. It didn't feel as urgent—I saw no immediate need to protect myself from anything or anyone. In reality, things were becoming more urgent than ever. From our beginning, I always kept a reserve of positive and glowing things to say about Wendy, to other people and to her. It was my all-in-one defense system and relationship growth promoter. I believe my simmering frustration-turned-resentment prevented me from tapping into that reserve. It was like closing the door to my broken areas but failing to engage the bolt. I was in danger and had no idea.

After 4 years in San Antonio, we were preparing for a move back to the D.C. area. I had finally applied for that doctoral program that was virtually impossible to get into, and I was accepted. The last step was an in-person interview at the University. Everyone celebrated as I left for an interview that was considered a mere formality. The Army chose me, the announcement had been made, and I received calls and messages from family and friends everywhere. They knew this program had been a goal for me since the beginning, and it was amazing to see it come to fruition.

The only problem was that the interview was not a formality—it had real implications. My interview started off well, but it became more intense with the entrance of one faculty member who asked some very tough questions. He seemed determined to derail what was turning out to be a great performance for me. I wasn't accustomed to rejection—remember, "no plan B"—so I left there believing I had done enough for a successful interview. I had not. I received a call days later to inform me that the faculty believed I needed more preparation before I was ready for the program.

I was devastated and embarrassed. I was also alone. Immediately after returning from the interview, I was back on the road for a months-long course in Kansas. I got the rejection call on the road. The faculty recommended I take a series of courses and then re-interview the following year. Just unbelievable. I already had orders to move back to the D.C. area to start classes. What would I do now? All those people were celebrating with me. What would I tell them? I decided I would contact everyone and let them know what had happened. I didn't want the slow and painful torture of people continuously asking about something that was now out of reach. I contacted as many people as I could to let them know there had been a change and to thank them for their support. That was hard.

> *1 John 1:8 (ESV)*
> *If we say we have no sin, we deceive ourselves, and the truth is not in us.*

During the same period of time as we prepared to move back to the east coast, I allowed myself to have conversations I would have never had, with people I would have never had them with at the beginning of my marriage. With my defenses lowered, many of the barriers I put in place disintegrated. I found myself in a place where there was a choice to make. I chose poorly. I cheated. The word "cheated" seems, in itself, an attempt to avoid the ugly truth of what it really means. I had sex with another woman who was not my wife. That is a profoundly painful truth to own, but it is my unfortunate truth. What I thought was a perfect marriage was destroyed in that moment. I had 100% of Wendy's trust. In that moment, I became unworthy of that trust. I thought that I could keep that secret and carry it to my grave. I decided that I would do just that. I had to reconcile what I had done with my reality.

How could I have made that choice?

Was I pretending to be someone I was not, over all this time? I walked out of the Walter Reed Chapel as the faithful husband who could only see his wife. That man seemed dead to me. I struggled with my choice and then decided. Obviously, I was still that broken young man from years ago. Clearly one woman was not enough, so I decided to accept who I really was and keep it secret. My life would continue as a masquerade, like so many of my family and friends had done. I allowed myself to get into another situation that would destroy my marriage if Wendy found out...

This is me now.

The new me...looking very much like the old me. But there was a difference. I could not live in peace with this version of myself. My wife thought that she was married to "Superman," and here I was...completely weak and meaningless. I couldn't live comfortably in that space.

I couldn't have her walking around and not knowing the truth and believing I was someone I was not. I couldn't sleep. I couldn't focus. I would have to tell her. I assumed the cost would be high, but there was no choice.

Our furniture was in transit, and we were living in a hotel for our last 2 weeks in San Antonio. I walked into that room after gathering my courage and prepared to deliver the news. But Wendy was watching an entirely different news story—Kobe Bryant.
The news had just broken that he was involved in a sexual assault case in Denver. His statement was that the encounter was consensual.

What??? Did he just admit that he cheated on his wife???

Wendy was H.O.T.! I was thrown off because I was not expecting this. Her emotion was strong. It's as if she knew Kobe personally and was directly impacted. If she felt that strongly about Kobe, what chance would I have? I decided my disclosure would have to wait for a while. Maybe forever.

The ride from Texas to Maryland seemed to go on forever. It was a trip of 2-3 days, with our 2 young daughters and 2 dogs on board. Over that entire time, I was feeling heavy with the weight of a secret I knew I couldn't keep. Our total conversation time was less than an hour over that entire 2-3 day trip. I think Wendy knew that I had something on my mind, but she didn't press for what it was.

We arrived in Maryland, dropped the kids off with my family for a week, and began painting our new home. We'd traveled back to search for a house several months before making the drive. Armed with paint brushes, wallpaper remover, and masking tape, we worked day and night to get the house ready for move-in. The weight of my secret grew unbearable for me. I had to tell her.

The moment came on the highway as we returned home from a shopping run one day. Why then? I just decided to say it. There was no safe place, no safe time, and no telling what the outcome would be. I just got up enough nerve to begin speaking...

"You remember when you said that if anyone messed up in our marriage, it would be me?"
"Yeah," she said.
"I have."
"What?" The look on her face was confused...intense...shocked...afraid.
"What do you mean?" she asked.
"I cheated."

Any magic remaining in our fairytale died at that moment. She was completed blindsided.

"Pull over."

I kept driving. We were on the highway moving at over 60 mph.

"PULL THE DAMN CAR OVER, NOW!"

I took the next exit and pulled into a parking lot. My mind was racing as I tried to figure out what I would do if she got out of that car. She didn't. As she escalated, I actually thought she might try to injure me in some way.

"How could you do this to me...to us...to our family?"

I had no response. What we had was perfect.

There was nothing I could possibly say to explain why I had destroyed our seemingly perfect marriage. I guess it wasn't as perfect as we thought. It was obvious...I was no Superman. I was just a man. Flawed. Weak. Foolish.

That moment was the darkest of my entire life. It felt like there was a hurricane raging, and I was adrift with no way to get control back. I was at the mercy of the situation. By violating my marriage, I had lost my ability to protect the peace that we had created together. On this day, there would be no peace. I don't know why Wendy stayed in the car, but eventually, we made it home.

Our conversation continued. The intensity of the moment was overwhelming. We were up well into the night. Every time I thought the worst was over, there would be a new surge of questions, tears, yelling...just raw emotion. All of a sudden, Wendy grabbed the keys and headed for the door. With blinding speed, she climbed in our SUV and peeled out of the driveway and out of sight. I didn't know what to do. I was horrified. I was afraid she might have an accident...afraid she might never return...afraid she might be running to someone else. I felt paralyzed and helpless. I knew that I was in over my head at this point, so I looked for help from the one person who I knew wouldn't judge me at that moment... my dad. I called him in tears..."I messed up dad. I cheated on Wendy."

Lowest point ever.

My father comforted me and prayed for me. Another moment of failure and he was there again. He helped me to keep it together and reassured me that Wendy and I could heal. I wasn't so sure, but I needed to believe him. Eventually, Wendy came back home. I was relieved, but I knew the road ahead would be long and tough...if there was going to be a road at all.

"Is there anything else I need to know?" she asked.

Wendy asked many questions over the next few days. Difficult questions. Direct questions. Repeat questions. I answered them all. At first, I couldn't understand why she kept asking questions, even when she knew the answers would be hurtful. It occurred to me that, hurtful or not, there could be no unanswered questions for her. She was trying to make sense out of what had happened, why it happened, and how it happened. I had to respond as long as there were questions.

We were sitting near the bottom of our steps in our dimly lit home one night. The house seemed really dark during those days. I don't know if it actually was. She said, "You are lucky I love God more than I love you."

I didn't know how to take that at first. What would I expect her to say? I was just wondering if she had enough love left for me to save our marriage. I was hopeful, but I dared not assume I was out of the woods. This journey was just getting started.

We hadn't even started our new jobs yet, and already the stress was high. And then, like a jolt of lightning, my insecurity kicked in. I started to feel threatened for some reason. Maybe it was because I knew Wendy had license to do whatever she wanted now. Or maybe it was because she told me as much. One day I picked up her phone and saw a message. That wasn't uncommon. We never had any reason to hide our devices. Then I noticed a series of messages from an unfamiliar contact. The voice in my head tried to slow me down...

Do NOT read those messages! You cannot unsee once you have seen.

As true as that was, I had to see those messages, so I tapped the screen. My stomach dropped and it felt like the blood rushed from my head and my extremities. Someone had come to town to see her...recently. Fear, anger, and despair rushed through me. Then the questions in my head hit...

Where did she go?
Who was it?
What happened?

I kept telling myself that I had no right to even ask questions.

You should be glad she keeps coming home at all. Do NOT ask her about anything you've seen. And do not look at that phone again.

I told myself I would not say anything to her at all, and I would avoid looking at her phone. The problem was that I was now consumed. I couldn't concentrate or sleep. I looked again. The pressure was more than I could stand, so I asked her about it.

Wendy denied my worst fears of an intimate exchange, but I didn't know if she was telling me the truth or not. Although I told myself I would not look at her phone again, that would work for only a day...maybe two. The silence was driving me crazy. Strangely, after she knew I read those messages, Wendy didn't lock or hide her phone.

Maybe she's using another account. I need to check her other email.

That is the moment when I knew I had to stop and my heart broke. I had to accept anything and everything, even the probable end of my marriage.

How could this fairytale be such a nightmare now? I was supposed to be this model husband.

Not only had I wrecked our dream, but I was now behaving like a jealous, controlling, and insecure man. That was not me. I had to get it together if this marriage had any chance of surviving. I had seen this scenario play out so many times, the end was predictable—a transactional relationship that requires verification of every move. No trust. If I had to verify her every move, there would be no way to re-establish the trust in our relationship. And what right did I have to do that anyway? I had to back off and let whatever happened happen. I was the one who had destroyed our fortress. If I had to languish in the rubble, then so be it. I resolved to never search her messages again. I had to give her room. I thought this might be it. I kept my anguish to myself and waited for the days to pass. I never searched her phone again.

I needed lots of help to keep my resolve and focus on saving my marriage. There were days when the urge to "investigate" was overwhelming. The silence was deafening.

Was she building the next chapter of her life, or was she working on us?

Was this dude checking in...coming to town...trying to build something...trying to dismantle the fragile remains
of my marriage?

It's what I would have done in his position. I was distracted and needed to get focused on the things I could still control before it was too late.

The war for our marriage was raging at this point, but Wendy and I were still together. That alone should have given me hope. But the real war—the one in my thoughts—was exploding and spiraling out of control: insecurity, jealousy, doubt, fear, anger, and despair. I knew that we could not recover unless I pulled it together. I prepared for my last stand. It was time for the church to become more than simply a place we went on Sundays.

Did you see anything you recognize?

My greatest failure came long before I violated the trust in my marriage. In many ways, a marriage is protected by a solid foundation, not great decision-making. Working on the foundation positions and protects us from having to face make-or-break decisions that impact our marriage. I was out of position in my words, my actions, and my duty to protect my marital space. I neglected the foundation I worked so hard to build. If you are at a make-or-break decision point, you might already be in trouble. Does your foundation need reinforcement?

When He helped me.

As Wendy and I were in our most broken place, we shifted our focus from each other and more toward God. It seemed that if we both moved closer to God, then we would move closer together by default. We were members of a church we both enjoyed—Celebration Church, in Columbia, Maryland. The people seemed genuinely loving, and we were more involved and connected there than any place we had worshipped in the past. At Celebration, we served in ways we had not in the past. Our connection to the church would be the lifeline that both of us needed.

Wendy joined the liturgical dance ministry—The Angelic Steps. I eventually got more involved in men's ministry. I needed more connection, support, and accountability with other men who were trying to live life in the way that I was—a way that was pleasing to God and worthy of my wife's love.

For her part, Wendy immersed fully in her dance ministry. Before Wendy joined, I hadn't realized that the primary function of that dance ministry was "ministry"—serving God and others through this art form. This was not dance for the sake of performing. This was something else completely. What the Angelic Steps did on stage was the outer expression of something divine and powerful happening during the time they "rehearsed." Those women created a space of spiritual growth, support, and love at a time that I believe Wendy really needed it most. They gave her something I could not give at that time. I didn't even know that Wendy could dance the way she did. It was beautiful. Every time she danced, I could see that Wendy was growing more relaxed. More present with God. Freer in her expression of His presence in her life and in her soul. She transformed. She was not just dancing…she was allowing God to use her through this artform, and she was emanating such a powerful energy in the process.

I began to form close relationships with some of the men at church. This required me to let go and take some risks. The more involved I got, the more I experienced the transparency and vulnerability required of real relationships between brothers. I discovered that we are all flawed, no matter how flawless we look in public. That was important for me. The guilt I felt was suffocating. The shame was worse. I thought that I had forfeited my right to happiness.

> James 5:16 (ESV)
> Therefore, confess your sins to one another and pray for one another, that you may be healed. The prayer of a righteous person has great power as it is working.

The Bible instructs us to forgive as we have been forgiven. As Christians, we do not have the option to hold people's mistakes over their heads. We are required by God's word to let things go and avoid holding grudges and throwing things in the face of those that have disappointed us or let us down. I was feeling sorry for myself one night when it hit me. I had to forgive myself. I didn't believe that I deserved forgiveness but realized that the same grace that covered everyone else's mistakes also covered mine. I didn't have the right to drown in guilt. That was important, because I had become tentative—reluctant to be the confident leader I had been in the beginning. Wendy reinforced that one night when she told me that she didn't need me to shrink away. She wanted the man she married. The confident leader who had no Plan B.

What??? She still wants me to lead?

We just might make it.

Until that point, I was not the man she married. My walk had changed. My presence had changed. I was a shell of my former self. No more. I stood up straight and fixed my gaze forward. Even when I didn't feel it, I straightened up and tried to pull myself together. I occupied that complicated space of owning my actions and their impact on my wife and marriage, while avoiding the tendency to beat myself up. It was difficult but important. I had to give Wendy the space to go through the process of healing in her way. She needed to know that I owned my actions, so that she wouldn't have to hold on to anything.

Whatever it took to heal our marriage, Wendy, and myself, I was willing to do it. I ensured that Wendy knew where I was at all times. I assured her that she was everything to me. Then I assured her some more. I focused on developing my own relationship with Jesus Christ. Going through the motions would not cut it. I needed a personal relationship with Him, and I knew that I had to submit my life totally to His will. I knew that I could not fix what I had broken, but He could.

Saving our relationship and having anything close to that magic we lost would require me to lean in and discard all pride and selfishness. The repair would need to be stronger than the original construction. How could I show her I was different? When you totally blindside someone because they never saw any threat in the first place, reassuring them that they can believe what they see—*this time*—is an enormous task. I needed Wendy to believe me again and allow herself to step out to take a chance. Again.

There were so many steps to that process, including giving her full-time access to all parts of my life and information. I ensured she had all of my email passwords, laptop computer access, and schedules. I registered her fingerprint on my cell phone and still do, to this day.

Michael E. Perry

No door could be closed. No place off limits. If Wendy wanted to walk in and look around, I had to ensure she could do that on her terms.

Many people—certainly men—would reject the idea of giving up their individuality in the way I chose to, but marriage requires a different mindset. A damaged marriage requires a revolutionary mindset—a God centered mindset. Individuality was not mine to have. If the "two" of us were truly "one"—as God designed marriage to be—then there was no "me." The two of us had to be one. No division, no secrets, and no words unsaid.

Pride says, "I'm grown." Humility and love say, "It's not about me and my rights. It's about the two of us and our life together." It's about sharing something that you've never shared with any individual on the planet. That is what I promised Wendy, and I was going to deliver. Still.

I realized I had so much to give to my wife that was unspoiled and still unseen by anyone on the planet. I could love her in the way that Jesus Christ loved the church—with pure love in action. Sacrifice. Grace. Humility.

> *1 Samuel 12:16*
> *Now therefore stand still and see this great thing that the Lord will do before your eyes.*

God revealed to me that we could still be blessed, despite my falls and failures. I believed it. Gradually, I saw flashes of something that felt like happiness between us. Hints of healing. Periods of peace and tranquility. Even with the occasional flare-ups or shutdowns, something was happening.

It would be misleading to suggest that everyday felt amazing. There were times when I would hear that voice in my head trying to say...

We should be over this by now. It's over and it's time she got over it.

I had enough presence of mind to quickly extinguish those thoughts. Every time. I kept telling myself…

Own it.

Healing, if it was to happen, would have to take the time it required. Not a minute more or less. That was not mine to define. Wendy was still there, battling for our marriage with me. I was determined to do whatever was necessary to rebuild our sanctuary. Pride and fatigue would block our blessing. Not this time. I had no idea what was to come next. Whatever "next" looked like, I was more committed than ever to doing life with this woman.

That was when our "second marriage" began.

God revealed the miracles he could work if we allowed him into our lives and our relationship. He gave us a marriage that was stronger than the "perfect" one we thought we had at the beginning. How could he use our broken and damaged pieces to create something stronger and more beautiful? Will you trust Him with yours?

When

Her Story.

Wendy M. Perry

Finding Myself.

I was twenty-six years old, smart, independent, accomplished, and alone. I was just a few years into my first military assignment at Walter Reed Army Medical Center, two years past my mother's untimely death, one year beyond a bad break-up with my then fiancé, and six months after having a lump removed from my breast. I was in a good place, but it didn't feel like a great place. I was still healing hurts, finding hope, and growing faith.

I grew up in a family of four: house, two cars, two kids, and a dog. We had a single- family home with a nice yard and a fence, and all seemed right with the world until it wasn't. My parents were married for 14 years, and I later learned that they had separated a time or two during that time for short periods, but somehow, I never knew that.

I also never knew about my half-brother, who is less than a year older than me—at least not until I was 9 or 10 years old. They loved hard, hosted parties, always supported family, and could not figure out how to not hurt each other. That all ended when I was 8 years old, and they decided to get a divorce. We said goodbye to the dog first…then the house…then my dad (the dog was the hardest part for me, at the time).

My mother raised my sister and me as a single parent for the next 4 years, then I said goodbye to my sister, who opted to live with my dad when she turned 18.

The 4 years after that it was Mommy & Me and then, after years of dating, she settled down with my common-law, stepfather. We had a relatively small family.

I grew up without knowing 3 of my grandparents. They died before I was born, so most of what I saw and learned in my formative years was from my mother and father's generation. They were young…and a little reckless. My father's mother died from cancer when I was 5 years old. She was not married and had two children with different fathers. My father had two half-siblings-one with the same mother, the other with the same father.

My mother had six brothers and sisters. On either side of my family there were only a few examples of an enduring marriage. The others were either divorced, had multiple marriages, or never married with kids. My sister married, divorced, and remarried. I don't believe my half-brother ever married, but at last count he had seven kids…I think.

My parents' marriage and divorce shaped my hopes and dreams for my own future as well. I didn't grow up with a dream of finding Prince Charming, getting married and having kids. I grew up wanting to be successful, not wanting to be on welfare, and being able to do it all on my own…just in case.

Something else happened that also shaped my hopes and dreams: when I was a young girl people often told me that I was cute or pretty and I would often receive a lot of attention. I started reading when I was two. I'm sure I was talking long before that and never stopped. When I was four or five years old, one of our neighbor's teenage sons would give me special, focused attention. He would always play games with me, and one day, a group of us were riding in the bed of his dad's truck going to a park or somewhere, he motioned for me to sit next to him. There were about five or six of us back there as we rode.

I recall suddenly feeling his hand rubbing my back…then I felt his hand slide down my back and into my underwear as he began to fondle me. Initially, I wasn't sure what was happening, but I knew that I didn't like it. I wondered if anyone else knew what was happening.

How could they not see? I moved away from him, quickly. I never visited their house again.

I would find ways of getting out of going along for visits or rides, but I never told anyone. And if I had to go to their house, I clung closely to my dad the entire time. That was a long time ago, and those memories remain vivid.

About a year or so after that, one of my cousins did a similar thing, but this time I thought this must just be how it is, so I went along with it. We had a house full of people over, which was common because my parents loved to entertain. My cousin told me to follow him, and I did. I followed him to my parent's bedroom and laid down with him on the floor beside their bed. He proceeded to pull my pants down and laid on top of me and right at that moment, my sister opened the door…we both jumped up and adjusted our clothes, and I knew instantly…that this was wrong. I was barely 6 years old, and I already knew all too well what fear and shame felt like, and regardless of how cute someone would say I was, I didn't feel as cute or as pretty anymore. Not long after that my parents divorced

When: Her Story.

and then, I knew disappointment. No more hoping or dreaming.

From the very beginning, I always excelled in school. I was active in anything that I could do that didn't cost too much or require my mother to be available- because she had to work. While she struggled to pay bills on a single income and raise two girls, she still managed to make Christmas feel like Christmas, and birthdays feel like birthdays. It wasn't easy.

We moved, on average, every two years util I left home to attend college. I attended three elementary schools, two middle schools, and two high schools. In elementary school I was a Brownie, a Safety Patrol, a cheerleader and was tested and placed in the Talented and Gifted program. In middle school I was in Chorus, Drama Club, and Science Club. I was voted "Best Dressed" (my mom's clothes) and "Best Looking". I wrote and directed my first play. In high school I played Softball, was in Drama Club, Student Government, cheerleading, Jr. Reserve Officer's Training Course (JROTC), and several other clubs and programs. I was voted on to the Homecoming Court as a Freshman and voted Best Smile as a Senior. I was also the highest-ranking cadet in JROTC and led the entire group. I have always been a leader. I stayed busy and enjoyed the recognition and accolades that came with it. I maintained Honor Roll status every grade, every quarter, every year. For as long as I can remember I also maintained a boyfriend. There was a short period of time in the 9th grade when I was actually juggling 4 boyfriends. It was kind of easy because 3 of them had the same first name, and that was cool…until I got caught. When I got caught, I was deeply remorseful, and regretful, and I vowed to play it straight after that.

However, in the next few minutes, 2 of the 3 called to let me know that I was forgiven and wanted to continue the relationship…so, I did…with both of them.

In 10th grade I had my first serious boyfriend, meaning that we did more than kiss. I trusted him, and I believed that I was in love for the first time. He was the quarterback of the football team and I was a cheerleader-textbook. He was charming and funny. With him, I had sex for the first time.

I was fifteen years old when I lost my virginity, and I was fifteen years old when I became pregnant. After that, I wasn't cute, I wasn't innocent, I wasn't pure. I had a secret that wouldn't remain a secret for long. He had no excuses, and no apology.

I didn't know what to do. I didn't know who I could trust. I didn't know where to turn. I imagined my parents' disappointment.

What would people think?

What would people say?

It was too much! I wanted to hide…I wanted to disappear…I wanted to just die. I felt so alone. I didn't have the baby.

My future was uncertain, and I couldn't see past my brokenness. The following year I gave my life to Christ and was "born again."

My mother and I moved in with my stepdad and I changed schools. It was a time of new beginnings. I was down to one serious boyfriend in my Senior year of high school, and he proposed toward the end of our Senior year…I said yes. We both had plans to attend college after graduation and we each had our personal struggle with making that a reality. I graduated with Academic Honors, but I was not a good, standardized test taker. I was a second-guesser…I still am.

Despite my proven academic record, I had limited options for college due to sub-standard test scores. No one in my immediate or extended family had attended college, including my sister, who is six years older than me and actually had the grades and test scores to go. She opted to join the Marine Corps instead. There were just the two of us…well two and a
half. I'm not sure if my half-brother graduated high school. I looked up to my sister who influenced most of my pursuits…she still does, and I still do. It was clear that my family could not afford to send me to school. I wasn't sure of my options, I could join the military like my sister, continue to work part-time jobs and figure something out, or find a way to go to school.

I was encouraged to apply to schools, and I did.

I was encouraged to apply for scholarships, and I did.

I was selected for a full, four- year, Army ROTC Scholarship under what was called the Quality Enrichment Program (QEP) which stipulated attendance to a Historically Black College or University. I was accepted to three of the six schools I had applied, none of those were where my fiancé planned to go. It was hard, but I had to consider what was best for me, even if it meant a long-distance relationship. I selected Prairie View A&M University in Texas and majored in Nursing.

Wendy M. Perry

It was a provisional acceptance, due to my test scores. and I had to take additional placement tests when I arrived — thank God I was better at those. I went to school in Texas- one thousand, five hundred and twenty-nine miles from home with no family, no boyfriend, and only two trips home a year — Christmas and summer break.

After my first year, I became a Cheerleader, and was voted Miss Army ROTC. I was back! I had proven that I could achieve academic success in college – despite what my test scores indicated. I was active and balancing schoolwork, activities, and dating.

Yes, I tried to remain faithful, but the time and distance encouraged us to grow. Unfortunately, we grew apart. I was already dating someone else when I ended the engagement. It was hard, but we both agreed — it was best. All was good until my third year in school...there was no Christmas trip home that year — I was devastated.

I had my own apartment, was working as a Nursing Assistant, and enrolled full time. Despite that, I still liked to go home, just to be a daughter, and reconnect with my friends and family. I failed two classed that semester. I was voted Class President at the beginning of my Sophomore year and re-elected as a graduating Senior, even after failing three classes. Although it extended my time in school by a semester, I made up the class, maintained my scholarship, and graduated with honors. I was selected to Preside over the Honor's Convocation for the entire University. It was a proud moment. With each success, I continued to slowly rebuild and believe who I was in Christ, despite my past. My mom and stepdad made the trip to Texas, for the first time, to attend my graduation and see my apartment. My father and sister couldn't make it. The next move was the Army, as a newly Commissioned Officer. I packed up and left Houston that summer and have only returned a few times since.

When I left, I had a serious boyfriend who was a year and a half behind me in school.
We decided to give the long- distance relationship a try and it seemed to work for two years. I would fly to Texas to visit or fly him to D.C. The second year after I left, he proposed…I said yes…again. As we shared the news with friends and family, it seemed everyone was happy for us.

Soon after that I found out he was cheating and had been for some time. I decided to forgive him and believed that we could make it work. I wanted to believe it. I wanted to believe that this was a mistake, and he would be true to me. I wanted to believe that there were men who didn't cheat, even though I hadn't met any, including my dad. My mother and sister supported my decision, and I was thankful for them. They each provided much needed comfort and reassurance in their own way.

Several months later, my mother died unexpectedly. She had a massive stroke from a cerebral aneurysm that was said to have been congenital — it had been there for her entire life.

Everything that I knew about my life and myself changed in an instant. It was a very hard time for me, I wanted to quit doing everything, I wanted the world to stop. I often said that home was where my mother was, and now I had to face the reality that she was gone. I had to decide between standing still and moving forward. I made the difficult decision to continue with my plans to travel for school and training, a few weeks after her funeral. It was hard, but I believed it was best. I was able to focus on work and was blessed to be surrounded by good friends and understanding mentors. Several months passed. My boyfriend and I maintained our distanced relationship and continued with our plans to get married.

As we began to plan the wedding, I discovered a lump in my left breast. A few years earlier my aunt, Beanie, had died from breast cancer. She was 37 years old. So many thoughts raced through my mind. My mind went from feeling a lump, to mastectomy and chemotherapy, in less than 10 seconds. I began to think that perhaps this was the result of things I had done in the past, to other people…to myself.

I built up enough courage to seek medical evaluation and tell my sister. I had a biopsy, followed by a lumpectomy, or more accurately, cystectomy. It turned out that there were actually two cysts. Then I waited. Waiting for pathology results is a harrowing experience. Every phone ring. Every email. Finally, I received the call…it was benign. It was not cancer.

> *Proverbs 3:5-6 (ESV)*
> *5 Trust in the Lord with all your heart, and do not lean on your own understanding.*
> *6 In all your ways acknowledge him, and he will make straight your paths.*

Thank you, God!

I tried to resume my life as it was and pick up where I left off. I tried to focus on the future that was decisively unwritten. I believed that God had spared me and had extended me grace. He *had* forgiven me, but I had not. I was humbled.

I was grateful. I made up in my mind that I was going to honor Him with my life from that point forward.

We continued with the wedding plans, but I thought it was a good idea for us to include God and get pre-marital Christian Counseling. He agreed. After we left the first session, he informed me that he was having second thoughts and that he felt trapped. Wait, what?

It was over. Really over.

At that moment, I lost that hope. I changed his flight and drove him to the airport the next day, I gave his mother's wedding ring back to him, and I didn't look back.

Although I knew that I had been forgiven, I was still dealing with the hurt and shame of my past. I questioned if I was worthy of finding true love and happiness…

Did that even exist?

Was it possible?

Did I deserve it?

When would it happen?

I was twenty-six years old, smart, independent, accomplished, and alone. I was just a few years into my first military assignment at Walter Reed Army Medical Center, two years past my mother's untimely death, one year beyond a bad break-up with my then fiancé, and six months after having a lump removed from my breast.

I was in a good place, but it didn't feel like a great place. I was still healing hurts, finding hope, and growing faith.

I was finding myself and discovering, not only what I truly wanted in life, but also what I hoped for and deserved in a husband. I allowed myself to hope. I allowed myself to dream. I allowed God to lead.

Did you see anything you recognize?

In this chapter, you were invited to witness the complicated beginnings of a young woman—one perspective on how early experiences play out in life over time. The parts of ourselves that we expose to other people are usually polished parts we allow the world to see. The interior can be much messier. Know that none of us escapes brokenness. For so long, I was held captive by guilt and shame. When I met Mike, I was on a path toward healing. I was finding myself, but the process was only beginning. As you reflect on the beginning of my story, I encourage you to stop here and take some time to reflect on your own. Are guilt and shame holding you captive?

When I Met him.

I didn't really want to think about dating at this point. I was beginning to gain some momentum in my career as an Army Nurse. I had an apartment, a car, and a cat (Simba). Life was good. I went on a few dates with men I met and some that I knew from years before, but there was nothing special or remarkable about them. I fell into what I will call my wind up and wine down days. My routine was easy, wake up, go to work, come home, eat and sleep. On my days off I would turn on some jazz, grab a glass of wine, and lose myself for hours in acrylics and canvas.

My apartment was perfectly appointed for me and my cat: parquet floors, black leather sofa set, entertainment center for my TV, stereo, books, and cassette tapes. There was a gallery of black & white photos of Jazz greats like Billie Holiday, Miles Davis and Dizzy Gillespie that lined the entry way wall. There was even a walk-in coat closet that made a great cat cave. It was a one bedroom with a shared living room / dining room and a separate kitchen, with French doors to conceal it from the main living space. My green Acer computer that my father bought me was housed in the corner of the kitchen, which was essentially the only reason I frequented the space at all — that, and a refrigerator.

One of the best features was my balcony. I lived on the seventh floor of my apartment building and it overlooked the Capital Beltway (Interstate 495). The Adelphi neighborhood in Silver Spring was tree-filled and always moving. Spring was green and Fall was fabulous with a refreshing array of the boldest reds and golds. I was conveniently 12-15 minutes from work and could jump on the highway in seconds.

I was invited to Church by a friend from work, I visited several times and eventually decided to join The People's Community Baptist Church. So, I was rooted and growing…and single…for the first time in a long time. Well…since first grade.

I have always loved to watch movies, likely because I had a small black and white television in my room from a very early age, let's say…3. I would stay up late at night and watch episodes of Perry Mason and the Twilight Zone, and I still enjoy a good suspense-thriller to this day. And oh yes…I am a Sci-Fi fan. I'm embarrassed to say that I caught far too many television signoffs which concluded with a waving flag, the national anthem, and static.

I also like to read. I wouldn't say that I am an avid reader, but when I find something that piques my interest, I can literally stay in one spot until I finish it. I, like many of my sisters, delved into the likes of Maya Angelou, Alice Walker, Terri McMillan, and others who validated our life experiences and provided both historical and contextual confirmation. Lessons in Living by Susan Taylor was one such book. I remember reading it and being prompted to really reflect on my sense of self-worth and identity, specifically at this point in my life.

After doing some soul-searching, I determined that I deserved better than a man who didn't value me, didn't encourage me, marginalized me, or cheated on me. Each of the men I dated, as an adult, had fit into one or more of these categories.

I accepted how I was treated and interpreted it as love. I accepted how I was regarded and interpreted it as respect. I accepted how I was cheated on and interpreted it as the norm. I wanted to be wanted and I needed to be needed all because I did not want to be alone.

I believed that my value was determined by how much someone else valued me. This was a life-changing realization.

So, I sat down one night and composed a list of all the things that I believed I deserved to have (plus a few that I just wanted), in a suitable mate- there were 27!
I wish I could find that list today, but for the most part I recall it. Here's the thing, I didn't go out looking for the rare and elusive man that was a match. I didn't go out looking at all. I prayed about it and let go of it. I had some real heart-to-hearts with God during this time. It was me, Him, and Simba, talking it up. Although I was alone, I was not lonely. I was at peace.

A few weeks passed. I had been recently selected for a new role at work that required I transition to another area of the hospital. The person who was leaving was orienting me. Along with the knowledge and resources that were shared, she also took time to introduce me to key individuals in specific roles within the hospital. On this day we walked into the office of the Hospital Commander, and there was a young man seated at a desk as you entered. I thought I had seen him once before, briefly, during the annual mandatory training sessions that we would have to endure to remain compliant with current facility standards. I noticed him and then he was gone.

This time, I saw him. He looked up and my eyes met his, and he smiled. We were introduced, "1LT Underwood, this is 2LT Perry, the General's aide." We shook hands, and she and I moved to the next person in the office, and then the next. We spent a few minutes there and as we left, I saw him again, typing. We said goodbye, I smiled…and we left. He was cute. There was something about him. I couldn't exactly determine

what it was, but there was something. I fully expected that I would be getting a call or some unrelated request following this chance meeting.

I didn't.

I concluded that he was either taken or was attracted to men. I laughed about it and moved on.

The unit where I worked had a very small staff and we were gearing up to run as a team in an upcoming 10-mile race, The Army Ten-Miler. We were short one person, and my friend suggested that I ask the young man I'd met in the commander's office. I told her she should ask him, since she knew him. She just gave me a look. I figured, why not? I emailed him the request…he accepted. He then proceeded to add… "by the way…you can call me Mike."

Really?

At first blush, I thought…

"Oh, the confidence," then I thought… "oh the arrogance." Nevertheless, it was a yes. The whole truth…I hated running! Now, however, I had something motivating me, and I couldn't let him down…I mean…I couldn't let the *team* down.

A week or so later, one evening, I was called to the room of one of my patients. When I arrived, I was surprised to find that she had two visitors, her husband, and "Mike (2LT Perry)."

They proceeded to introduce us to each other, and we shared that we had already met, briefly, a week or so earlier.

Now things were getting a bit interesting. They simply said that they believed that we should meet. To this day, they take credit for introducing us and so does my friend. Interestingly, the chance meetings became more frequent, and our paths seemed to cross often. Finally, after several weeks, he called to the unit, asked for me, and informed me that he had something that he needed to deliver in person on behalf of someone else. Truthfully…I was eagerly anticipating his arrival. He came to the unit and our whole team was there to meet him. He gave me what he came to give and expressed gratitude on behalf of the commander's wife, and then, before leaving, he asked if we would like to join him for lunch. My co-worker declined. I accepted. There really was something about him. However, I refrained from getting excited about this guy. I was cautiously moving forward in my mind. I was in a very interesting place in my life, and as I shared, I was not actively looking for someone to fill the void.

I remember a conversation I had with my dad around that time, we talked about many things, openly. I told him about a few of the guys I had dated and described the journey over the past year, and then I told him about "Mike." I simply said, "I don't know…there's something about him." My dad told me to go with it. I was still tentative, and truthfully, I was guarded.

Ultimately, I went with it! We went to lunch at the Woodside Deli, I ordered an open-faced turkey sandwich, and to this day, it was the best sandwich I have ever had. We had lunch, and I couldn't stop thinking about him. All I could think about was what would come next.

I wanted to call him, but I thought that would be showing my hand. I was giddy…but cautious. I was hopeful…but tentative. I was beginning to gain some momentum in my career, I had an apartment, a car, and a cat (Simba). Life was good. I went on a few dates with men I met, and some that I knew from years before. There was nothing special or remarkable about them, but there was something about Mike.

He was all 27 things, plus a few. He was tall, dark, handsome, gentle, caring, strong, smart, and funny. He was athletic, and he was fit. He had a great smile, though his eyes showed a little pain and experience. He had hands that were strong, as if he was not a stranger to work, but gentle enough to type with precision. He was charismatic and polite. Did I mention that he was smart? He was all about family, and he was a Christian. He grew up in the church and was not embarrassed about it. He liked to eat crabs. I don't want you to miss that one…he liked to eat crabs! He could dance. He looked great in just about anything. He could drive, he had his own car. He had his own apartment. He had a great job and a promising career.

He was careful and he was deliberate. He didn't like cats...nobody's perfect.

He was too good to be true...and it was too good to be true. It was a dream until it wasn't. A few weeks in, we couldn't get enough of each other, we talked non-stop, and days turned into nights that turned into days. I felt so comfortable with him, and we were comfortable with each other, as if we had known each other a lifetime in just a few weeks. We went to his apartment and he asked for a kiss...I said no...because he asked me, tentatively, instead of proceeding with confidence...I needed him to be certain.

That was the last time he asked for a kiss. I recall that his phone was suddenly very active...buzzzz...and a few minutes later, another...buzzzz.

This continued for most of the time we were there. He finally checked it, left briefly to check in with his roommate, and it was time for us to leave. We left, and I later learned that the calls and texts were warnings that his recent ex-girlfriend, was in route. Yes, you read that correctly.

Insert drama.

I had no idea that there was an ex, let alone, recent ex, and that she was not in total agreement with being an ex. I learned that she knew who I was, and that Mike and I were beginning to date. I repeat...I had no idea that there was an Ex.

The ride was over...let me off.

The walls and doors that I had carefully constructed and intricately built, that I was beginning to deconstruct and slowly open, came crashing closed and reinforced in an instant.

How could he not tell me?

How could he allow me to walk around unaware that she knew who I was, but I had no idea about her?

I was right about that first meeting…he was taken. I, very calmly, told him that I liked him a lot, but that he needed to take some time to get himself together before calling me again. I had been through too much heartache, disappointment, and pain in my life already. I was not going to willingly walk into more. Just like that it was over.

When I met him, I didn't really want to think about dating. I wasn't looking. I was finding myself. I was hurt, but I was healing. I was single, but I was no longer alone.

Career, car, cat…you know the rest. He was, and it was, too good to be true. And now it was, and almost was, a happy ending, love story, that ended before it really got started.

Did you see anything you recognize?

The beginning of healing is just that…a start-point. Decisions and behavior can change instantly, but sometimes it takes life a while to catch up. There are no short cuts. I wanted something different for my life, but I had to do all of the work required to prepare myself and my space for the change. Have you started the work required to prepare yourself and your space for change? Have you given your cares and desires to God?

Wendy M. Perry

When I Loved him.

There was something about him, but I quickly got over it.

Not really.

I couldn't believe I was here. It all felt real. I wanted it to be real. It *was* real. A few weeks passed and I missed him, but I didn't call him. I meant what I said…no matter how hard that was. I didn't know what would happen next with us, but I moved forward with me.

Then he called. I melted.

He called, he explained, he apologized, he assured, he confirmed. I answered, I accepted, I believed, and I trusted. I recall that when I saw him again, he had the most amazing roses I have ever seen, and they lived for a long time, and even grew! I was still cautious, but I was in…all in. I had to confront the fact that although it had only been a brief, few weeks, I loved him.

Was it love at first sight? I wouldn't necessarily say that, but there was something. I had been in several relationships. I had been engaged twice. I knew what love was and what it felt like. I also knew what it wasn't. What was different? With him I felt safe.

Once rekindled, our relationship grew, quickly and deeply. We picked up where we left off and I never looked back. I loved this man and almost everything about him! Every love song or love story had elements of what we were experiencing. I learned that he could cook. Man could he cook, he could sing, he could iron, and sew. The fact is, I continued to learn something new about him and I still do. After a few months, a call from my ex, a car accident, an epic evening that included a chartered plane, a Halloween party to remember, the best crabs in history, and memorable dates to some of D.C.'s most historic and popular sites, he told me he loved me.

I responded, "Okay."

I was all in, but I was still guarded. I knew that I loved him, but I wasn't ready to surrender that. Not yet.

The car accident. I was on my way to the hairdresser, in preparation for the epic evening I alluded to, and as I was proceeding to turn left at an intersection, a car across the intersection impatiently went around the car in front of him and ran straight into me. This was my first major accident, and I was a wreck…literally. I was upset, I was scared, I wasn't really injured (that I could tell), but my car was undriveable. I called my dad and he talked me down.

It's funny when I think about it. Whenever I was afraid, stuck, hurt, or needed help, the first call was always to my dad. After I composed myself and my car was towed, I proceeded to walk the rest of the way to make my appointment…priorities. As I sat there a million thoughts crossed my mind, but the one that matters is that I wasn't sure who I could call to come get me. My father suffered from what was believed to be amyotrophic lateral sclerosis (ALS), otherwise referred to as Lou Gehrig's disease. Mentally he was sharp, but he was physically incapacitated. Watching the gradual decline in his physical condition was difficult, but his mental faculties remained intact. My father was my friend and my confidant. He was the person who could help me calm down with only a few words. He was my first call after the accident happened… Mike was my second.

I wasn't sure if this was the right move at that point, but I made it. He came to my rescue! He arrived shortly after I called and waited for me until my hair was complete. If I had any doubt before then, I absolutely knew that I loved him now. Needless to say, I actually *was* a little banged up, but nothing was going to keep me from that date. It did however keep me from the event that brought us together…The Army Ten-Miler. I wasn't upset about it.

We continued to date, and it felt as if everyone around us was rooting for us. We would meet for breakfast, and lunch, then we would have dinner together, and it was as if the days were all one continuous experience. On the weekends, we would go on a date, he would bring me home and then he would stay. This continued for I don't know how long. Then somehow weekends became weekdays, and although he doesn't like for me to describe it this way, "We were shacking up." For Christians, premarital cohabitation, and more specifically, fornication, is a sin, period. We both knew this. So, for Mike, we weren't living together. He denies it to this day, qualifying it by the fact that he never had a key. As for the other thing…well let's just say that lying is also a sin. We actually took our time and really got to know each other before taking that deep dive. We talked about it, but we held on to our virtues…until we didn't. Sex can complicate things, especially feelings. I loved him before I knew him.

I said to Mike, many times since, but for the first time, that he "may not be perfect," but he was "perfect for me."

When: Her Story.

He really is. In so many ways.

Everything that I dreamed of in my perfect mate, he was. There was very little not to love about him. This is not to say that we were a lot alike. In fact, we are very different. We have similar likes and interests, but we are different, very different, and I loved even that about him! I would say that he fell for me pretty hard and fast, and I don't believe that was his plan. I think that what we both found was unexpected, but we knew what it was, instantly. He was all in. Definitely, all in. I don't think there is anything that he would not have done for me then, and I don't think that there is anything that he wouldn't do for me now.

It was pretty early in our relationship when I met his family. We made the drive to Virginia for a Halloween Party and it was a party I will never forget. I'm pretty sure everyone was in costume and they were their authentic selves. It was refreshing and familiar all at the same time. His family made me love him more. His sister had just had a baby a few weeks earlier, and it was a very special time. When I saw how gentle and loving he was with his nieces and new nephew, how much he loved and adored his family, and how close they all were, I wanted to be part of that family. Honestly, that was the first time I had that feeling…ever. I think they accepted me too, with the exception of a skeptical few, and a few that were holding out hope that Mike would reunite with his ex. I learned that a little later. I passed that test, and they passed it too.

When he met my dad, it was hilarious, my dad was in rare form. He would raise the head of his bed up, to ask a question, then he would lower it down as he waited for a response. This continued for at least 10 minutes, then he let

Mike know that he was just messing with him. My dad had a sense of humor that is rare. He went right at him though and asked him/us where we thought the relationship was going.

Whoa, whoa, whoa!

It occurred to me that my dad had not met any of my other boyfriends, I didn't consider that at the time, but it is true. I'm not certain that any of them would have passed the test...Mike did.

Days became weeks, weeks became months. We had the occasional challenges of a "feeler" phone call or gift from an ex or close friend. We had the holdouts. We had a few minor tiffs. For the most part we were able to navigate those unscathed. Getting your family completely on board is a challenge that many couples face, especially if they had a close relationship with your ex, or if they believe that they know what is best for you.

I sometimes wonder how many relationships have died because they were unable to overcome parental or sibling bias. It began to look like we were in it for the long haul, even though we had not discussed it definitively. We talked about marriage, we talked about children, we talked about a lot of things. Somewhere in the midst of those conversations, we started to move...closer to each other...and closer to the idea of marriage. One thing we both agreed on is that when we got married, it would be once and that it would be for life. I'm not sure if that was confidence or arrogance, but we were certain, despite having only a few marriages between both of our families and friends that held up to that standard.

I did not want the story of my marriage to reflect the stories of the marriages that I had seen growing up. I believed that my story, my marriage could be different. I was thankful that my soul-searching, self-reflection, and prayer had led me here. I was grateful that I had been blessed to meet someone who was everything that I that I thought, dreamed, and prayed for. I loved him. I wanted to marry him, but I was not yet brave enough to fathom it. I expected the fairy tale, but I anticipated the nightmare, and that lasted for a long time. I wanted to believe, I wanted to trust.

Would this time be different?

Would I find out there was another ex?

Would he also feel trapped?

> *Psalm 37:4 (ESV)*
> *⁴ Delight yourself in the Lord, and he will give you the desires of your heart.*

I made every effort to go with it and trust God for it, but I struggled. I was able to bring myself to a place of being able to receive and accept what I was being given.

A few weeks later, we had a little "heart-to-heart" over a gift he received from a "close female friend." Okay, so it was more than a heart-to-heart…it was a major argument. I think the issue we were arguing about wasn't the *actual* issue. It was that I felt he wasn't telling me everything…again. That he was only sharing certain details. At this point we were in pretty deep.

I let him know that I wasn't okay with it, then I drank one, two, and then half of his favorite beers. I don't even like Heineken.

Then my phone rang. It was one of my old friends from school, and I proceeded to tell him what was happening, loud enough for Mike to hear. I was really putting on a show, and now, as I think about it, it was so unnecessary. I think I wanted to see how far I could push it…how far he would let me go.

After my rant I went to sleep. Mike woke me up and then he…he proposed. In the middle of the night, early in the morning. I remember it well.

He said, "I promise to make every year better than the ones before it, if you will accept me, I want you to be my wife."…or something really close to that. Lionel Ritchie, "Just to Be Close to You" was playing softly on my stereo, and it was very still and dark.

Initially, I said nothing.

Then I said yes!

All of my apprehension, my questions, my guardedness, my walls, and doors vanished. I trusted God in this and that made this one different. I couldn't believe I was here. It all felt real. I wanted it to be real. It *was* real.

Did you see anything you recognize?

What is influencing your actions and decision making? Is there any such thing as waiting too long or moving too quickly to get married to the one you love? How often are your decisions driven by people and circumstances outside of yourself or your relationship? Who determines when the time is right for you? If there are more than two people in your decision-making process, there might be too many.

Wendy M. Perry

When I Married him.

It had only been 7 months. We dated for 7 months. That first introduction was sometime in July of 1997, and we began corresponding and talking on the phone in early August. Our first date was sometime in late August. Then it was over in early September…and back on late in September. I met his family in October, and he met my dad. He "unofficially" moved in early in November. He completely won me over with bread made from scratch for our first Thanksgiving together. It was February when he proposed. Then he asked my dad for permission. It was like something out of a movie. My dad said something that day that I often reflect on. He said, "Make sure that you both know where you are going and that you are both going in the same direction."

We planned our wedding in less than a month and we were married on April 4, 1998. Talk about a whirlwind. During that short time, we experienced love, restoration, change, and loss. We were tested, and we discovered that we were a good team. That together, we could overcome anything. That's how it felt.

Our timeline was shortened because we were both on assignment to Korea and we determined that we wanted to go overseas as husband and wife. There really was no good reason to wait because we knew. I believe that even if that had not been the case, we probably would not have delayed much longer. I knew that Mike had been God-sent and I believe that he believed the same about me. After I said yes, I was worry-free. It was as if a burden I had been carrying was lifted. I was free to hope, free to dream, free to love without boundaries or restrictions. I felt as though I had known him my whole life and I was excited to get to know him more. I felt closer to him than I had ever been to anyone and I could not have been more certain about anything.

A few weeks before we were to be married, Mike's grandfather passed away. I had only met him once — briefly at Mike's promotion ceremony a few months earlier. It devastated his family. Although I had experienced death and loss, all too frequently in my family and at work, Mike had not. His immediate family had not. I only knew one of my grandparents — my father's mother — and she died when I was five years old. In contrast, Mike knew and grew up with all of his grandparents and was well into his twenties when his grandfather passed. He was navigating this for the first time.

We weren't sure if we should postpone the wedding, but with deep reflection, thought, and prayer, we decided to move forward. The funeral was held on the same day that my Bridal Shower had been planned, and Mike urged me to attend the shower. I did, but I felt that I should have been there with him. I still do.

We were able to grieve this deep loss and anticipate our future at the same time. This wasn't the first time that I experienced these parallels. Just as I had with my mom, we moved forward with our plans, despite the loss and

> *Genesis 2:24 (ESV)*
> *24 Therefore a man shall leave his father and his mother and hold fast to his wife, and they shall become one flesh.*

pain, and perhaps in some way, we were fueled by them.

The topic of pre-marital counseling came up and I had a flashback…oh no! I've been here before…but this was different. Mike's uncle was a Pastor and had agreed to marry us, but he required that we go through the counseling before he would perform the ceremony. I believe we were his first marriage ceremony, and he was serious about the process. We went to his house and he invited us to the basement where he commenced to share with us the importance of understanding the commitment, we were about to make to each other and to God. He made it very clear that this was a covenant, not a contract. It was both terrifying and comforting. We completed the required counseling, and with his blessing, we were ready.

We were married in the historic Walter Reed Memorial Chapel. It was quaint, it was ornate, it was perfect. It rained that day. ALL of his family was there, some of my family was there, and many of them were late. I sat in a limo just outside the front of the church and watched with anticipation as our families and guests arrived. After the last few scurried in, it was time.

My sister and I walked up the steps of the church and Mike's dad met me at the double doors that led into the sanctuary. Mike's dad walked me down the aisle and I recall it as if it were yesterday…the music began—it was Mariah Carey's "Whenever You Call," and as we stood waiting at the back of the church, my father-in-law was nervous and excited. He kept wanting to go, but we hadn't reached the part in the song that we rehearsed that we would walk on. He kept saying, "Whenever you're ready, I'm ready." I think he said that at least three times and then we took that first step.

As the song played, I was living and breathing the lyrics…

> *Love wandered inside*
> *stronger than you, stronger than I,*
> *and now that it has begun,*
> *we cannot turn back*
> *we can only turn into one…*
> *and I'm truly inspired,*
> *finding my soul there in your eyes,*
> *and you have opened my heart and lifted me inside,*
> *by showing me yourself undisguised.*

My eyes met Mike's, and I held that gaze the entire time. He was so handsome, so tall, and so strong, and I loved him! Mike's dad handed me off to my dad, who was wheelchair bound. In his motorized chair, my dad rolled hand-in-hand with me the rest of the way, to give me away to the man who would become my husband. I was shaking.

I don't think I was nervous…I was certain. Nevertheless, I was shaking, and I couldn't stop. My Mother-In-Law sang the Lord's Prayer, and her rendition is unrivaled to this day. There are many details of the day that I recall with total clarity, and I could recount them; however, what I remember the most is the look in Mike's eyes…the tears that welled in them…and the overwhelming feeling of love that I felt as we entered our covenant between us and God. It was as if there was no one else in the world, but us two. It was the happiest moment of my life. As we turned to face our families and friends as husband and wife, it truly

Wendy M. Perry

felt, for the first time, that it was us against the world and that I had a partner for life. As we left, I never looked back.

I have only a few memories of our reception and mostly because they were captured by photos and video. The first and perhaps one of the most important is that I forgot the CD that we were supposed to dance the first dance to. I really didn't have to do a lot on my wedding day except get dressed and be ready…and bring the song. I had one job! Somehow, in my preparation and travel, I left the cassette at my apartment and didn't think of it until the very moment that we were being announced for the historic first dance. The song was "Meet Me on the Moon" by Phyllis Hyman. We had only been married a few hours and I had already let him down. It wasn't my intent, and he was forgiving, but the memory remains. You might be thinking, *it was just a song,* or *anyone could have forgotten.* Both of those are true, but for me it was otherwise a perfect day, but for one little mistake. The truth is that there were many things that went wrong that day, but it didn't matter. I was marrying my best friend, and I didn't want to let him down.

We made it past the first dance and then I danced with my father. I sat across his lap with one arm around his shoulders as he whisked us away and around the dance floor in his motorized chair. It was magical. Just as it had been moments before, it felt as if no one else was in the room, but us. It was an endearing moment that I will always cherish. My mother had passed away just two years and eight months prior, so I didn't get to share this day with her, and it was bittersweet for me. I felt her there with me, but it was bittersweet, nonetheless. My sister was in our wedding as well, she was the Matron of Honor, so I was not alone. I didn't get to attend her wedding because it was in Hawaii. My mother couldn't go either, so neither of us were there. I can only recall attending one wedding in my entire family before my own.

The following morning, we were awakened by a knock at our hotel room door…it was Mike's dad.

I can't recall exactly what the visit was about, only that he came in, sat down, and got comfortable. We laugh about that to this day. I knew that marrying Mike meant marrying his family, and I knew how close they all were, but this was unexpected. Mike was the first of his siblings to get married, so I was his dad's first walk down the aisle. From that moment to this, I became another daughter. I didn't feel like I was part of the family, I felt that I *was* family, and that continues. We repaid the favor a year later when his dad remarried, we dropped by for an early morning visit, and it was equally…no…more uncomfortable.

The next several weeks seemed to fly by as we prepared to begin our married life together in Korea. There was planning, and packing, and more packing. We decided to sell Mike's car and put mine in storage while we were overseas, to save money and make it easier on our budget. As he drove his car to the dealership, I followed close behind. This was one of the first big decisions for us and it was exciting!

We were a few minutes away and…BAM!!! I was hit by a car. This was my second major accident in less than a year, and I was a wreck…literally, again. It all happened so fast. I looked up and I could see Mike's eyes in his rearview mirror. I thought I had died. He looked terrified. Next, I remember seeing him running towards me. There was smoke, the smell of chemicals, a lot of noise, glass, and people. The airbag had deployed, and my right knee was bleeding. All I remembered from before the crash was that the car coming from my left had a signal light on- but didn't turn, and once I started into the intersection, it was too late. It was a father and two children, a boy, and a girl. I was so concerned for them…and they were okay. Mike opened the front passenger side door of my car, got into the seat, and asked if I was okay. I said, "Yes, I think so." He then said, "I just have to ask you this question…did it hurt when the airbag came out?"

I smiled.

An ambulance arrived and my car was totaled. I had only known him for 8 months, and in that time, I had my first and second car accidents. I can only say that it was good that he came along when he did, both times he was there to catch me. I was a little banged up, but I was safe.

We were married on April 4, 1998. Talk about a whirlwind. During that short time, we experienced, love, restoration, change, and loss. We were tested, and we discovered that we were a good team, and that together, we could overcome anything. That's how it felt.

Did you see anything you recognize?

The early years of a marriage can feel like a roller coaster ride or a rocket ship. Our experience was a bit of both. Blending two lives into one is a challenge, and with each added variable the challenge grows more complicated. I often wonder if the volatility in our first year eclipsed other seemingly insignificant issues that we might have addressed under normal circumstances. Some of those issues were hidden…waiting to emerge when the dust settled. Is there anything waiting for you?

When he Hurt me.

What started as a Fairy Tale, seemingly too good to be true, continued to defy our pasts. The early years as husband and wife were in no way what we planned or even anticipated. To be honest, I am not sure what I expected, but I knew that it wasn't what we got. We were so ready to begin our lives together and almost instantly, we were separated. We arrived in Korea full of excitement and hope and in 24 hours, our hope was dashed. We had anticipated working in the same place before we arrived, only to be told that Mike's assignment had changed, shortly after arriving. My birthday was the next day, and that year I was sad.

The next several months were spent apart during the week and together for two days on most weekends. Oh, how I anticipated the weekends! My landlord would call to me— "Ahjumma! Ahjumma!" (Korean for a married woman)—to let me know that she could see Mike coming up the road, followed by excited pointing and, "Ajusshi! Ajusshi!" (Korean for older man/Mister) She didn't speak English and I didn't speak Hanguk-eo, but we understood each other. I think she was just as excited as I was.

After a few weeks of getting settled in Korea and our routine, we bought our first puppy—a Bichon—at a street market. We named him Kimpo after the local airport, and he kept me company during those long weeks. He was the tiniest, cutest, fluffiest little thing, and I loved him immediately. Pets were not allowed into the country without having to endure several weeks of quarantine and vaccinations, and I decided that it was better to give

Simba, my cat, to a loving family before we left, versus putting both of us through that.

I had left him once before for a few weeks, and he didn't talk to me for a least a week and scratched up my couch.

After several months, we reached the season of Chuseok (or "harvest") and decided that the timing might be right to start our family, despite advice to enjoy being husband and wife and married life for the first 5 years before having children. It was sound advice, but we chose to ignore it. I think I recall saying something like…

"We have too much love to give to keep it for ourselves."

About a month later we discovered that we had succeeded. I was pregnant! It was an exciting time!

In almost one full year, we met, dated, married, moved, and now we were expecting. A few weeks later, we learned that Mike's cousin, who was like a sister to him and had been diagnosed with cervical cancer shortly before we left, was succumbing to the illness. We did everything that we could to return home before she passed but were held up by what the airline described as unavoidable delays, that to this day, still cause us to hesitate when selecting that airline.

One full year, two close family member deaths, where there previously had been none for Mike. This was really hard. A few weeks later, I had a miscarriage. It became harder. I blamed the Army and the anthrax vaccine…I blamed myself. I felt that I was suffering alone, but I could see and feel that I wasn't. Mike was able to spend some time with me and away from his job and I appreciated that

When: Her Story.

so much. He helped me heal, even when I didn't believe that I could. That time reminded me that I was not alone and of that feeling that together we could overcome anything.

We certainly had our share of challenges, and we were still newlyweds. Despite the separation, distance, weekend rendezvous', and losses for both of us, we grew closer and stronger together and to God. A few months later I received a call that my dad was in the hospital. We flew home again. For both of us to get approval was rare for a one-year military tour in Korea.

When we arrived, my father was despondent and was not responding to anyone. Everyone was concerned. I spent many hours at his bedside and even bathed him and brushed his teeth. Mike helped. The next day, he started to come out of whatever had affected him, but he was still not quite himself and I was deeply concerned. A few days later he was recovering and at home, but still not quite himself. He was confused, and he was mean. I wasn't okay with leaving him this way, but I was reassured by his progress. I had a hard heart-to-heart with him, and we left. I was thankful for the time we spent. Despite his condition, it was not wasted. After several days, he made a full recovery and had only a vague memory of our visit and his hospitalization. I often encourage people to appreciate the time they have with their loved ones. Whether you are recognized or remembered by them, the true value is in the moments that you are able to share — not the memories of them. A month later I was pregnant again.

When we returned permanently to the U.S.A. after our Korea assignment, we had a dog and a baby on the way!

We were headed to Texas and new beginnings. We bought our first house, started new roles at Fort Sam Houston, TX, and were well on our way to starting our marriage and family in the way we had hoped. God blessed us with our first daughter, Sydni, 1 year and 9 months after we were married.

I recall that one couple that mentored us and advised that we should wait 5 years before having children because they knew our lives would be forever changed, and with that knowledge, I would do it all over again the same way if given the chance. Our lives were changed and somehow now had more meaning. We were off to a strong start, and things were going well. We found a local Church, a good daycare, and we were moving up the ladder in our careers.

One Sunday at church, I noticed someone that looked familiar, but I couldn't quite place her, it was Mike's ex. OMG! First it was church, then it was at the gym. I could not get away from this person. One blessing that I had not realized up to that point was that our year in Korea was a year away from our pasts and the people in them. It is easy to focus on each other when the distractions of former relationships are in another country! As much as I like to believe that moving forward means no looking back, that is easier said than done. Especially when those old flames keep popping up.

We continued on our trajectory for the next few years and continued to grow. Two and a half years later, there were new jobs, new roles, and a new baby — Morgan. We had successfully breast-fed, potty trained, and won the battle of sleeping in your own toddler bed for our first born and were excited to try our hand with the next. We also got dog number two, "Q."

Yay for me…boo from Mike!

Those first two years were not without incident, and it required an adjustment for all of us. There was getting used to a new body, a new baby, and trying to achieve work-life balance. There was hearing the child fall down the stairs and not being sure who was at fault for not securing the gate. There was being too tired to cook, or clean, or anything else—if you know what I mean—but being expected to anyway. About that... when we met,

I didn't cook and hadn't really cooked for myself before meeting Mike. I knew how to not starve, but I really didn't have a love of food prep and meal prep. Mike seemed to enjoy it!

> *Philippians 4:12 (ESV)*
> *12 I know how to be brought low, and I know how to abound. In any and every circumstance, I have learned the secret of facing plenty and hunger, abundance and need.*

He did most of the cooking, if there was cooking to be done. I recall that we had conversations about it, and I had always anticipated that when I had to provide meals for more than just myself or the two of us, that I would make the adjustment. I nursed both girls for at least 9 months, and after that it was easy to buy baby and toddler foods. So, my adjustment was slow. What I couldn't appreciate was my husband's expectation that I would adjust sooner and transition faster and would do my share of cooking. This became and remained an area of tension and contention for us. It still, sort of, is, but less so. This became "The Dreaded Conversation" for us and remained so for a number of years. Other than that, it was all good.

Wendy M. Perry

We were young, we were successful, and we were on the go. Up until then we had been blessed by not being separated for any extended period of time—not more than a week or so. We were establishing ourselves in our respective careers and were embarking on the next big moves. Mike had applied for graduate school, and we were anticipating relocation.

As he left for his final program interview, we were all but assured of what and where that would be—back to D.C.! He did the interview en route to extended training that would have him away from us for close to four months. He returned briefly after the interview and was soon off again. Unlike many military families who have had to endure deployments and extended separation, we really had been blessed to both be assigned in the same location and not be deployed in those early years. The separation was hard, but not impossible.

Then an unanticipated outcome. We were notified that he was not accepted into the program following the interview, and we were both devastated, but we were separate. My heart ached for him. We had been on a World Tour of congratulations, only to face rejection soon after. I applauded him for his courage and character during that time. This was a man who had no Plan B and had not needed one. He personally contacted every person that congratulated him and, with humility, informed them of the final outcome. I was so proud of him.

It is in moments of adversity that true character is revealed. I wanted so much just to hold him and comfort him. I hoped that my love and words would be enough. I also knew that he would not be gone forever. We made it

When: Her Story.

past that, as we had so many challenges up to that point. When he came home, he was different…distant. Hardened in some way. It was interesting because Morgan, our youngest daughter, took a while to warm up to him again when he returned, but she was still an infant and that quickly waned. In the next few months, we were headed to D.C. and his plan was to take the advice he received, to take a few classes, and re-apply…and he did.

We were off, to return to Maryland where it all began, and were eager to begin the next chapter. We hit the road with two kids, two dogs, and a bunch of stuff.

The drive from Texas to Maryland is long. This drive was longer. Something was bothering Mike, and I wasn't exactly sure what it was. I assumed that he was still sorting through his feelings related to graduate school. We only talked a few minutes for the entire trip. We arrived in temporary housing in Maryland as we awaited moving into our next home. A few weeks passed, moved in, and were settling into our new home and new jobs. Then a conversation happened that would change everything. As we were headed home one evening, Mike said these words…

"Remember when you said if something went wrong in this relationship that it would not be because of you?"

I said, "yes."

He proceeded, "You were right, I cheated."

It was as if someone had punched me in my chest. It was hard to breathe. I think I blacked out. I was completely blind-sided, and I wasn't sure I could handle it.

I asked him to pull the car over, because I honestly wasn't sure that I wouldn't punch him in the face or choke him, and I had to consider the kids in that moment. He didn't immediately do as I requested, so I said it again, LOUDER!

"PULL THE DAMN CAR OVER NOW!"

He took the next exit and parked the car. He commenced to explain to me what happened. I imagine it was like having
an out-of-body experience, as if I was watching myself and us. I was utterly devastated.

How could this man that I love so much do this to me?

How could he do this to us?

Why would he hurt me?

How could I not know?

How could he be so selfish?

How?

Why?

When?

> **Mark 10:9 (ESV)**
> ⁹ *What therefore God has joined together, let not man separate."*

Spin. Spin. Spin.

During that time some of Mike's family were coming for a planned visit. I prided myself on being a great hostess and welcoming everyone into my home- this time was different. The last thing I needed during this crisis was a visit. I had always said that you wouldn't see a smiley face on my door if it was not a happy home.

I never wanted us to be falling apart but faking like we had it all together- I had seen that all too often.

Here we were.

When they arrived, I didn't even go to the door. When I pulled myself together enough to greet them, it was without my signature smile-I couldn't. It was without warmth-I had none. I didn't even ask how they were doing-I didn't care. I didn't fake it.

My sister-in-law immediately sensed that something wasn't right, and she asked me if I was okay. I said "NO!" We went outside and talked, and I told her everything…tearful, embarrassed, and exhausted- everything! Her response shocked me, she said…

"I can't say I'm surprised…no wait…I am surprised it took this long."

What!!!!

She then proceeded to share that she knew her brother very well, probably better than anyone, and she knew *who* he was before he met me. Which is why she was not surprised, but she was upset, very upset! What she said next may have been the one thing, at that crucial time, that kept me from packing a bag and leaving. She said…

"I know that you are hurting right now, but one thing that I know for sure is that Mike loves you more than anything or anyone!"

She was right. At least, I wanted to believe it. I believed it.

The one thing that I never questioned, even in this, was whether or not he loved me.

What started as a Fairy Tale, seemingly too good to be true, continued to defy our pasts. The early years as husband and wife were in no way what we planned or even anticipated. In all honesty, I am not sure what I expected, but I knew that it wasn't what we got.

Did you see anything you recognize?

Our vulnerability made us susceptible to breaches in our marriage long before Mike violated the trust in our marriage. We were both out of position to protect our marital space. We were made more vulnerable primarily because we trusted more in ourselves and each other than God. In many ways, a marriage is protected by a solid foundation, which is the covenant entered into when vows are exchanged. From the beginning God is in it, we determine whether or not He is in the background or in the forefront. What is your marriage based on? Does your foundation need reinforcement?

When He Helped me.

There are times in life when we recognize that we are unable to do things under our own power. That it requires something greater than us to act or move. This moment was that time for me.

I didn't know how I would get past the hurt, the pain, the betrayal, if getting past it was what I was supposed to do.

I didn't know how I could forgive this, if forgiving was what I was supposed to do.

I didn't know how I could look into Mike's eyes and not feel pain for the rest of my life.

I didn't know how to believe that our marriage would be different, when we were entering the same trap that my parents and his parents…that my family and his family had before? I didn't grow up with a dream of finding Prince Charming, (but I found him), getting married (but I did), and having kids (I had two). I grew up wanting to be successful, not wanting to be on welfare, and being able to do it all on my own…just in case.

Was this the "just in case?"

What had been modeled for me did not include forgiveness.

It showed me bitterness.

It showed me resentment.

It showed me anger, hurt, and revenge.

When: Her Story.

I didn't deserve this…I also didn't deserve grace!

Whoa.

See, I made many mistakes in my life. As a young girl, I was pretentious and promiscuous. I was manipulative to people who were younger or incapable of defending themselves. I lost

> *Ephesians 1:7 (ESV)*
> *In him we have redemption through his blood, the forgiveness of our trespasses, according to the riches of his grace*

my virginity at 15 and was pregnant at 15…and elected to have an abortion. I slept with a former boyfriend, even though I knew he was married. I cheated, I failed, and I lied…except for grace. It is also true that I was molested when I was 5 years old, and that may have influenced my promiscuity, but I knew it was wrong. I was very smart and mature as a young girl and that may have caused me to use this ability to influence others. I came from a divorced home and moved homes and schools every two years, which may have caused me to search for love in the wrong way.

Despite everything that I had done, everything that I had thought, everything that I was, and everything that I am…God loved me.

God loved me.

God loved me.

His hand was at work from the very beginning. I would trip, and He would catch me. I would fall, and He would pick me up. I would try to throw it all away, and He saved me.

He saved me.

He saved me.

There I was, realizing and recognizing that I was unable to do anything without Him. At that point, during this time of reflecting, replaying, and ruminating, I finally decided to *truly* trust and follow Him.

I professed my faith and belief in God when I was 16 years old. I believed that I had been forgiven for my sins. I knew that I would not live a sinless life—although I could try. It was after being saved that I would trip, and He would catch me. I would fall, and He would pick me up. I would try to throw it all away—again and again—and He saved me.

He saved me!

He saved me!

I was never promised a life without pain or tribulation, but I wanted it. I was hurting, deeply. I couldn't fathom that this man that I loved so much would do this to me, to us, to our girls. I realized in that moment that I had put more faith in him than I did in Him. I had grown to trust and believe Mike more than I trusted and believed God…but…I loved God more than I loved Mike, and I was reminded of that. God loved me, and He knew my needs, my desires, and my pain. God brought this man into my life…for life!

I knew that Mike had been God-sent and I believe that Mike believed the same about me. I had said many times, "though he may not be perfect, he was perfect for me." He really was, still...even in this.

Everything that I dreamed of in my perfect mate, he was... still.

Yes, he cheated. Yes, he hurt me. Yes, he regretted it. Yes, he told me. Yes, he loved me...still.

Had I made mistakes? Yes.

Had I let him down? Yes.

Am I saying that I played a role in his decision to cheat? No.

It was *his* mistake. It was *his* sin. He had to own it, repent, and ask God's forgiveness. My forgiveness of him was optional. I had to search my own heart. I had to repent and ask God's forgiveness. If there was ever a time when I needed Him, it was then.

I prayed and I cried, and I cried, and I prayed, until there was nothing left for me to do, but be still and know. I trusted God in this and that made this man, this relationship, this marriage, different. I couldn't believe I was here, but I was.

It all felt real.

I didn't want it to be real.

It was real.

Had our fairy tale become the nightmare I anticipated?

Should we have waited those 5 years before having children?

We had been through so much in such a short time, and together we had overcome it all, but we needed God to overcome this, and we both knew that.

I decided to forgive him.

With that decision, I knew that I was forgiving him for everything that he confessed and even for what he hadn't. The days and weeks that followed were hard. I would search for the strength to smile, but I couldn't. I considered revenge, but I couldn't follow through with it.

There was an email from an old college boyfriend, followed by a phone call from that old boyfriend, followed by a visit with that old boyfriend. I agreed to meet him with every intention of paying my husband back, but there was something in me that would not allow me to do it. My flesh said yes, but God said no. I had to choose not to become what I had seen, but what God had purposed for me. I was not living my mother's life, or my father's life, or my sister's, or my friends'. This life is my own.

For the first time in my life, I asked other people to pray for me…for us…for my family. I started to read God's word, seek God's face, and to worship. I was blessed to be invited to minister with the Praise Dance Ministry at our church, The Angelic Steps. I had enrolled the girls in the School of Dance for several years and had often considered making myself available, but often made excuses. It was time to say yes. These women embraced me, prayed over me, and helped me heal. I found peace in these moments to move forward.

I believe that one of the reasons this happened in our marriage, perhaps, was to align my faith. *Everything* that happened in my life served to align my faith, my purpose, and to lead me back to Him.

So much of what I focused on, up to that point, was dependent on myself or other people and not God. This was true at home and at work. When I sincerely surrendered it all to Him, I found peace. I still struggled. I still struggle. The days and weeks that followed became easier. Once I accepted that my joy and peace were not dependent on my husband's behavior and choices — or my children's behavior and choices — I was released, and so were they. I could not have arrived at this point under my own strength or my own understanding.

He helped me.

He healed me.

He saved me.

As I reflected, I realized that I put a lot of effort into being the best nurse, wife, and mother, I could be. Everything I did was for my job, or my husband, or my children, or my family. I wanted to be perfect in everything, and I worked hard at doing everything that I could to get close. I'm not sure if I was trying to make up for my past or if I was just driven. I thought that everything that I was doing was the reason that I had the life I had…that my successes were my own. I discovered that it was not because of what I was doing, but because of what God was doing. I put a lot of things before God, and this experience reminded me that I needed to keep God first.

Then I forgave myself.

Without faith, I would have succumbed to the pressure.

Without faith, my marriage would have ended.

Without faith, my life would have ended- at my own hands.

For the next few years, I focused on God, believing God, and trusting God in all things, especially my marriage. I did not cheat. I did not leave. I did not sleep in a separate room. I did not pretend that nothing had happened and that nothing had changed.

> *Matthew 6:33 (ESV)*
> *33 But seek first the kingdom of God and his righteousness, and all these things will be added to you.*

We *were* changed. I was changed, and in some ways, becoming better. Slowly, I started to believe in us, again, because He helped me. Slowly, I began to have renewed hope for my marriage because He helped me. Slowly, I began to believe in myself, again, because He helped me.

There are times in life when we recognize that we are unable to do things under our own power. That it takes something greater than us to act or move. This was that time for me. I didn't know how I would get past this, if getting past it was what I was supposed to do. I didn't know how I could forgive this, if forgiving was what I was supposed to do. I didn't know how I could look into Mike's eyes and not feel pain for the rest of my life…but God.

That was when our "second marriage" began.

God revealed the miracles he could work if we allowed him into our lives and our relationship. He gave us a marriage that was stronger than the "perfect" one we thought we had at the beginning. How could he use our broken and damaged pieces to create something stronger and more beautiful? Will you trust Him with yours?

remember when...

This book takes you on our journey. We want you to take some time to remember and reflect on your own journey together. For each of these events: *Think*, *Write*, & then *Share* with each other. Have fun with it! Pull out old photos or videos.

♡ you first met

when

where

how

♡ you dated

first date

favorite place

favorite song

♡ you fell in love

when

where

what was it about him?

♡ you got married

when

where

what was the best part?

We encourage you to make time to be together, just the two of you, for the specific purpose of remembering when...

Mike & Wendy

About the Authors

Dr. Mike and Wendy Perry founded Catalyst Executive Advising and Development in 2015 as a platform to shift the culture of organizations around the globe. They transform good leaders into exceptional leaders—people experts who value relationships, build trusting teams, and enjoy extraordinary performance and results. With over 20 years each of leadership in the U.S. Army and in communities worldwide, Mike and Wendy retired as senior officers—leveraging unparalleled training and real-world experience to give all leaders access to effective approaches for overcoming adversity and emerging at the top of their game.

Mike holds a Ph.D. in Clinical Psychology and a Master of Science Degree in Medical Psychology from the Uniformed Services University in Bethesda, Maryland. He is also a graduate of Georgetown University's Leadership Coaching Certification Program and the Practice of Adaptive Leadership Program at Harvard University's Kennedy School. Wendy holds a Master of Science Degree in Nursing from the University of Maryland, with Certification in Health Services Leadership & Management. She is also a graduate of the University of Georgia's Sherpa Executive Coaching certification program, and Cornell University's Women in Leadership and Diversity and Inclusion certification programs.

Mike and Wendy have been married for over 23 years and are the proud parents of two beautiful daughters. They serve together, leading several local and regional ministry organizations and activities. Most recently, Mike and Wendy joined FamilyLife's Weekend to Remember speaker team, charged with teaching and sharing Biblical principles for marriage with couples nationwide. They also currently lead a virtual Marriage Ministry, "The Marriage Shop" via Facebook and YouTube. You can catch them on Mondays at 7pm Eastern.

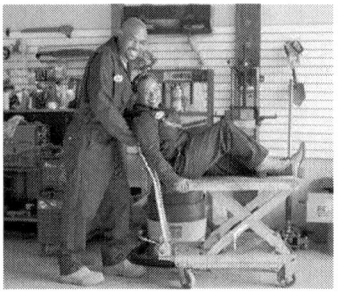

CONNECT WITH *US*!

Mike and Wendy Perry

available at amazon

And now these three remain: faith, hope and love. But the greatest of these is love.

1 CORINTHIANS 13:13

Made in the USA
Middletown, DE
13 October 2024